SHEPHERD'S
SIGHT

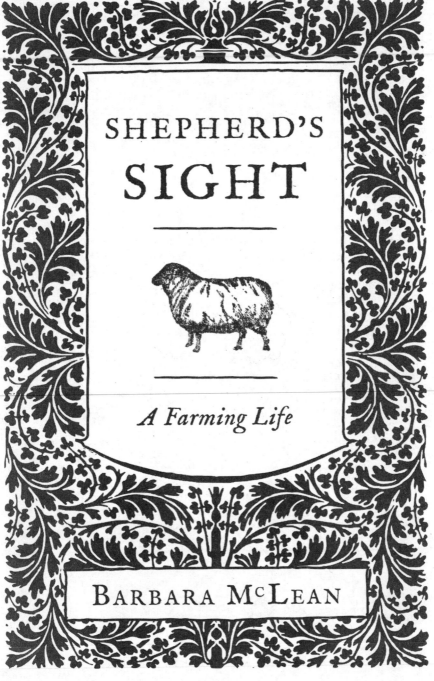

SHEPHERD'S
SIGHT

A Farming Life

BARBARA McLEAN

Published by ECW Press
665 Gerrard Street East
Toronto, Ontario, Canada M4M 1Y2
416-694-3348 / info@ecwpress.com

Editor for the Press: Jen Knoch
Copy editor: Crissy Boylan
Cover design: Jessica Albert

To the best of her abilities, the author has related experiences,
places, people, and organizations from her memories of them.

LIBRARY AND ARCHIVES CANADA
CATALOGUING IN PUBLICATION

Title: Shepherd's sight : a farming life / Barbara
McLean.

Names: McLean, Barbara, 1949- author.

Identifiers: Canadiana (print) 2023058568X |
Canadiana (ebook) 20230585698

ISBN 978-1-77041-765-6 (softcover)
ISBN 978-1-77852-291-8 (ePub)
ISBN 978-1-77852-292-5 (PDF)

Subjects: LCSH: McLean, Barbara, 1949- | LCSH:
Women shepherds—Ontario—Biography. |
LCSH: Shepherds—Ontario—Biography. | LCSH:
Sheep ranchers—Ontario—Biography. | LCSH:
Sheep farming—Ontario. | LCSH: Sheep—
Ontario. | LCSH: Farm life—Ontario. | LCGFT:
Autobiographies.

Classification: LCC SF375.32.M35 A3 2024 | DDC
636.20092—dc23

This book is funded in part by the Government of Canada. *Ce livre est financé en partie par le gouvernement du Canada.* We
acknowledge the support of the Canada Council for the Arts. *Nous remercions le Conseil des arts du Canada de son soutien.*
We acknowledge the funding support of the Ontario Arts Council (OAC), an agency of the Government of Ontario. We also
acknowledge the support of the Government of Ontario through the Ontario Book Publishing Tax Credit, and through
Ontario Creates.

PRINTED AND BOUND IN CANADA

PRINTING: FRIESENS   5 4 3 2 1

MIX
Paper from
responsible sources
FSC® C016245

For Ian
and
Alistair

"Sheep may safely graze and pasture in a watchful shepherd's sight."

— Cantata BWV 208, J.S. Bach

Contents

Prologue

My small sheep farm lies nestled in the undulating terrain of Ontario on a landmass edged by three of the Great Lakes. For half a century, I've been learning how to live on it. And in it.

For when I arrived, with my partner, Thomas, the buildings were practically derelict. Nothing improved, nothing modernized. We should have had more skills to take it all on, but we were young and naive enough to think we could stretch ourselves, to root down into the rich soil, to reach up toward the highest barn beam, to openly embrace a community and way of life unknown to us.

Moving in mid-winter, in a blizzard, I first learned how to survive without central heating or hot water. Without so many things. But with painstaking effort and thinning patience, I worked feverishly through those first twelve months to make improvements while trying to learn the rhythms of the agricultural year.

Now decades later, on a summer day if clouds are just so, heavy and dark draped over gossamer dew, I muse at my farm window and imagine myself back on the west coast of Ireland where the idea of my country life was born. The rolling hills here are reminiscent, the stone walls similar, and sheep season every field they graze like grains of salt.

I could be looking through a smaller window in County Sligo, my elbows on its wide stone sill, my chin in my hands, gazing out at the Irish mist. Rain softly rolled off the packed stems on the thatched roof; it made no sound. Even hail bounced in silence. Then the sun returned; steam wafted into the air and floated into the distance. Behind me, the flagstone hearth edged an open fire. The chimney widened above a grate and andirons; pothooks held the black kettle and flat griddle. Glowing turf scented the air.

Overwhelmed by the need to make things after months of roving, of hitchhiking from the Pacific to the Atlantic, flying from Newfoundland to Scotland, hiking the highlands and moors, camping in remote fields with ewes and newborn lambs, I pitched up in a borrowed cottage on the west coast of Ireland. A vagabond looking for respite. I craved to settle, to create comforts and substance from raw ingredients.

I was anguished then by political unrest. American Civil Rights marches, Vietnam protests, Quebec separatist violence, the Irish Troubles to the north. I wanted to opt out of the establishment. To shed my suffocating, claustrophobic upbringing of bourgeois manners and formal dining, where books were a waste of time. I felt neither accepted nor acceptable to my family. Instead of doing something they considered productive, I spent hours in the library or in my room reading or scribbling. I felt almost deliberately misunderstood in an emotional wasteland, a stifling atmosphere where strict rules and outward appearances trumped affectionate relationships. They distrusted me, thought me radical, read my private diary, tried to break my will.

I found respite with a much older neighbour. She was an avid reader, a brilliant thinker, an attentive listener. An educated intellectual, she understood and acknowledged me, introduced me to a sophisticated world of obscure music and books. She fostered my love of animals with her menagerie of dogs and cats, gave me hope for a different kind of future. I was a cuckoo in the nest, and it was time to fledge. In Ireland, I decided to change my life: to leave the city behind, to slow down, bake bread, make jam, knit socks, read books, have animals. To risk an uncertain path.

On the wettest of the wet Irish days, I stayed in the cottage, boiled the kettle over the fire for tea, knitted with local wool, read poetry and local history, formed rough loaves to proof on the hearth. I experienced the peace that Yeats says "comes dropping slow / dropping from the veils of the morning." When the rain was sporadic or misty — what the Irish call a "soft day" — I ventured to the water's edge, watched the tides as they gathered and dispersed. At low tide, I collected mussels, brought them back to steam open over the turf for a succulent supper garnished with tiny pearls.

I baked Irish shortcakes on the griddle. Flour mixed with lard, dotted with currants, rolled and cut into rounds, flipped over the peat and laced with its scent. And there were potatoes. Tender, exotic, rich with flavour and texture, they bore no resemblance to the lumpen fodder from my youth. These were growing tubers, freshly harvested from rich earth, their skins red and gold and thin as gauze.

I learned how they grow, ventured out into the rain to follow the thin roots underground to the prize, and left the plant to make more. I weeded a garden flourishing with vegetables, with rhubarb and gooseberries for my jam. To pick the berries, I approached from the top of the drystone garden wall, lost my footing, and fell right into the bushes. I learned that gooseberries have thorns.

I was enchanted with this wondrous place of solitude, this place of solace after my tempestuous childhood, my dissenting adolescence. A place I could live for a time mainly off the land: the produce in the garden and the orchards that others had planted and tended, the wild food of the tide. That summer, I learned I could live in quiet and isolation, my only neighbours the sheep on the hills, their lambs at foot. I learned to love a garden and to harvest and transform its produce into succulent, simple dishes.

And now in midwestern Ontario, where I have been raising sheep and lambs and growing a garden of my own for half a century, I realize the importance of that Irish summer in directing me back to the land, showing me a way to live. As I look out my kitchen window, if the clouds are just so, I catch a spark of those early days yearning for change, and I remember what brought me to this pastoral way of life.

My years on this farm have been rooted in the agriculture calendar, in a shepherd's calendar — governed by the whims of nature, by the seasonal cycle of sheep fertility, by the arrival and departure of frosts, the whelping and weaning of coyotes who threaten my flock. Each and every month signifies an age-old phase in the farming calendar. And over my years here, though the implements and methods have changed, the constant flow of breeding and birthing, sowing and haying, harvesting and reaping follows the sun in a yearly orbit, ending only to begin yet another round. And for as long as I can, I will move with it, month by month, season through season, shepherding my flock.

January

The loft is cold as the year turns over. A chilly draft seeps between the gothic windows and their storms, nothing quite fitting tight. The peaked ceiling has just a thin layer of insulation between the paint and the cedar shingles, and the whole north end is glass. A chimney runs through the space, its parged sides stingy with the heat within, but some warmth wafts up the stairwell from the wood stove below.

The wood is wet this year. Soggy from a summer of alternating showers and monsoons. Wood that was stacked to dry, piled north-south so the prevailing westerlies would whistle through, instead sagged from so much rain. The fires are slow to start. They sputter and die down, the heat evaporating in the sap.

Mice inhabit the house. A tiny house mouse, fearless, runs along the walls of the kitchen, into the front hall, hides in the toy tractor shed made from a clementine box. A perfect Beatrix Potter house. He is part of a family. I hear them in the walls and the heating ducts, and in the mornings I find their tripped traps, empty, safe still. My pantry is littered with tiny bits of foil, bitten off the tops of olive oil bottles. They prefer the first press.

Outside all is avian. Woodpeckers — hairy and downy —
peck the house if I run out of suet. They suss out cluster flies from
under the eaves and attempt to exhume the desiccated corpses
trapped between the window panes. Goldfinches and chickadees
are the January mainstay. Blue jays intermittently chase them off,
then depart in frustration as the feeders shut with their weight.

The barn is quiet in January. Sheep are on maintenance: fed
hay in the morning, hay in the evening. That's all they ask. They
are content to munch, ruminate, gestate, and stay outside in the
courtyard, despite having access to the barn. Snow covers their
backs, but wool traps their body heat. They begin the year placid
and calm, undeterred by blizzards or sleet, sensing perhaps that
they will be cared for. Fed and watered. Greenwood, the calico
barn cat, lies curled like a comma in her straw nest under a feeder.

We moved to the farm in January fifty years ago. Young enough
to weather the ruin it then was. It was storming as we drove the
rented truck with all we owned up the snowy lane. I don't remember the cold that day. Perhaps the furnace had been installed by
then, but I do know there was no duct work yet, nor hot water,
nor anything but basic electricity. Excitement and possibility must
have kept me warm as we lit the wood-burning cookstove in the
primitive nineteenth-century kitchen.

With youth and energy in abundance, we took on the task of
creating a proper home and farm from the ruin of this acreage. The
house had long been neglected, and January was clearly not the
best month to move in, but Thomas had work in town, and January
was when it began. He was at home until the middle of the month,
and together we scraped and cleaned and shivered and coaxed the

workers who were hired to update the house with a bathroom, a kitchen sink, hot water, heat. There were delays. Setbacks. And even with the blessing of nostalgia and fading memory, I can recall the frustrations and the fears that this was an idiotic plan to move to the country, some miles from the village, even more from the small town, a place where we knew no one.

The book-lined loft I sit in now was uninhabitable then. Dark and dank, it was windowless but for a tiny square of glass at the north end, completely obscured by cobweb and flyspeck. The stairs were rickety, the walls and ceiling unfinished, and just a few boards covered the floor joists. It sat above the back kitchen, a precarious wooden extension of the house used only in good weather for canning and jamming, for sifting summer breezes and keeping the heat of the summer cookstove away from the main house.

By the time we arrived, the summer kitchen's doors were askew on their hinges; there were holes in the floor and rusty tin tacked to the cladding. We were advised to pull it down. But after a few years of using it for muddy boots and whelping pups and little more than a bulwark for winter north winds, we propped it up, rebuilt the stairs, finished the walls and ceilings, and laid the floors.

And I sit in my loft now and ponder what brought us here, what made us think we could create a life in this relic of a farm, this brick tent of a building.

※.※

Thomas and I met on a blind date in the autumn more than fifty years ago. I was merely seventeen, still living with my parents, and visiting friends at a university a few hours away from home; they set us up. Thomas, a medical student, was twenty. I returned a few more times that year, and in June he said he'd see me that summer. I was hopeful.

Three years later, at a summer wedding in South Wales, we saw each other again. He was the best man, sent over from Canada by friends to stand up with his college roommate, who had just finished graduate studies at Aberystwyth. The ceremony was mostly in Welsh, the final guests chosen according to their singing voices. Hymns rang out in five-part harmony. In Welsh. As I was staying in the U.K. that long vacation, I was invited to attend. One of the few Canadians to witness our friend's marriage to his Welsh bride. Thomas was resplendent in his Moss Bros. tails, eloquent in his speech.

There was another woman, someone he had travelled with the previous year. At the after-party, she fawned; I demurred. I took myself off toward my room upstairs in the inn, when suddenly he was there in the foyer behind me.

❦❦

The following morning was our first journey together. We left the small Welsh town of Ammanford and hitchhiked to London and beyond, staying in bed and breakfasts, walking on walls, travelling footloose and free before returning to Montreal in September. It was 1969.

After university, we returned to the British countryside on holidays, stamping through Dorset, camping in the Scottish highlands, becoming acquainted with footpaths, with farm fields, with sheep. Lambs woke us at four in the morning, bleating helplessly at sunrise, frantic for their mothers. I warmed to their cries.

In Canada, we travelled from sea to sea, through vineyards and orchards, prairies of waving wheat, pastures of livestock, hitching rides and camping at sunset. Farming seeped into our veins by osmosis.

When we reached the end of the road on the east coast of Newfoundland, we flew directly to Scotland, switched to the other side of the road, and thumbed our way to Holyhead, sailed the ferry to Dublin, and begged rides to Sligo Bay, where a friend lent us her three-hundred-year-old thatched cottage, and I began to learn to live on the land.

After years of study, hours spent in libraries finishing my literature degree, brutal twenty-four-hour shifts for Thomas as a junior doctor, we were ready to withdraw, to find a plot to plant and tend, a house and barn to revive and fill, a life farming, and a future fuelled by strength, by youth, by naive dreams.

꽃꽃

Before my children were born, my days were filled with renovation of the house, the barn, and the garden. I spent hours scraping away layers and layers of wallpaper inch by inch in every dilapidated room. I knocked down a wall to make a bigger room, then had to plaster the hole I'd created, using antiquated tools to sand my rough work. I worked room by room, trying first to prepare a comforting place to sit and read in the evenings, somewhere out of sight of the incessant jobs still to be tackled. Somewhere I could escape for a few hours into poetry and fiction. As the weather improved, I spent more and more hours in the barn. Not just repairing and fixing, but preparing for livestock. I read everything I could find about small-scale farming, took courses at the agricultural college, and watched the animals in my neighbours' barns. I took careful note.

If I were to have sheep, I needed to learn to work with wool. My grandmother had taught me to knit when I was small. I was already skilled with needles, two or four or five. But I needed to learn to spin and weave, to acquire a wheel and a loom if sheep were going to be my future.

One of the workmen who helped rebuild the loft, the one who kept telling me to tear it down and start over, mentioned a woman on the next concession who was a spinner of fibre. I knew of her, but we'd never met and were unlikely to. So one day, when I recognized her in town, I followed her home, drove right up behind her in her laneway, and boldly asked her about spinning. She graciously took me in, showed me her spinning wheel, demonstrated her skill, and let me try. The fleece fell apart in my hands; my feet could not get the rhythm of the treadle. She told me about courses at the technical college not too far away; I enrolled for a summer session — one night a week.

It is a frustrating process, learning to use the foot treadle steadily so the wheel glides slowly and continuously, to hold the fleece lightly so it doesn't over-twist or pull away and break. I spent hours just treadling. By the end of the course, I had my own spinning wheel; I could fill a bobbin with lumpy yarn, fill another, and then feed them through the orifice again, spinning the wheel in the opposite direction to create a two-ply yarn. If I wound it off and twisted it into a skein, it looked almost presentable. By winter, I had made Thomas a pair of chunky socks, my first finished work.

I was filled with excitement at being part of a back-to-the-land movement, at getting back to the garden. Most days, it was everything I had imagined. No gritty city streets, no crowds, no boss. My timetable moved with the sun and the seasons. There was so much to learn, but I had generous neighbours, a good library, and when I failed at something, I took Beckett's advice: tried again and failed better.

I came to farming with absolutely no training. My childhood was spent in a pleasant town close to a large city. It was big enough to be urban and small enough to walk everywhere. The countryside was close but foreign territory, viewed from the car window. I couldn't identify crops or cattle breeds; there were no sheep.

My mother's meals were plentiful and delicious; she could make anything from scratch. But she was delighted not to in the early days of prepared and packaged products. I never saw her bake bread or make jam. She grew only mint and chives. I learned to cook from Fannie Farmer and Julia Child. And to preserve from my rural neighbours.

Those nearest to us, on the farm around the corner, took me on as a kind of apprentice. Though she cooked all the meals, processed all the produce she grew, Maik was no farm wife stuck in the house; she drove the tractors, hauled the hay, milked the cows, mucked out the pigs. And she had me doing all of those things over time, frequently laughing at my ignorance. Hands-on time in their barn, shovelling manure, gathering eggs, feeding calves — those were the tasks that taught me what I needed to know.

She and Gerrit had a difficult lifestyle — never a day or evening off from barn chores — and I know money was tight and treats were few. They were both small in stature, azure-eyed, incredibly strong. They always worked together, and brought up their children with the independence of self-sufficiency.

Theirs was a mixed farm, something that has all but disappeared. They milked about twenty Holstein cows with an old-fashioned milking machine that had to be moved from cow to cow down the line, then manually emptied into the separator. The cream brought a constant paycheque; the milk fed the pigs and calves. Hens, geese, ducks, and many cats and dogs roamed the barn, even pheasants some years, emus. But there were no sheep.

When we asked a nearby farmer to sell us some ewes, he declined, saying his flock was only a sideline for market lambs, and put us onto another neighbour who had some excellent stock to sell. How lucky we were to be introduced to Fred. He was a retired Royal Canadian Mounted Police inspector and had the posture and bearing one might expect. A kind and gentle man, he and his wife, Bertha, had returned here from the city years before to buy back the farm she had grown up on. They had sold most of their flock of Hampshire ewes but had kept a few favourites while they were in the process of switching to Corriedales, a New Zealand breed with finer wool.

I knew little about wool then, only that I wanted to grow some of my own. The Hampshires are a handsome breed with a springy dense fleece which grows down around their black faces and legs. They are blocky sheep, a leg in each corner. Prolific with lots of twins and triplets, they are a prized meat breed. And they are pretty. Their lambs start off black and adorable. It seemed a perfect choice for us.

Although he wasn't a handspinner, Fred loved wool, perhaps because of the iconic uniform of the Mountie, the red serge wool tunic. He was an expert and bred his flock for beautiful fleece. He cared for his animals with diligence and wanted his Hampshires to go to a good home. I must have passed the test, because I became the proud owner of four named animals of varying ages: Old Spot, Susie, Hampy, and Blackie.

Fred taught me to be a shepherd. He was always there to help in a crisis, to lend a hand or a piece of equipment. He shared his years of experience willingly, and over the years, as he aged, I was able to give back by helping in his barn, watching over his flock if he had to be away.

The work was hard and often discouraging, but my farming neighbours became my friends, and their tenacity and encourage-ment gave me strength. And does still, if only in memory.

In the early days, I was happy being alone full time on the farm, working here and helping my neighbours, Maik and Gerrit, and learning from Fred. I had no children; my time was my own. I had not expected to want to be a mother. The 1960s and early 1970s were a time of radical political and cultural change. There was war and revolution and a huge backlash by the young against the status quo. The future often looked bleak. It did not seem to be a good time to bring new life into the world. And despite some pressure to have babies, I was doubtful of my parenting ability after enduring a strict and difficult childhood. It seemed a big risk to take. But after five years of delivering lambs, watching their dams taking such immediate and careful care of newborns, I was surprised to feel a biological pull to have babies of my own.

Through my own pregnancies, I began to see the ewes differently, to relate to their lumbering bodies, their awkward shifting to find a comfortable position. I felt an unborn lamb kick when I rested my hand on a ewe's flank as my own fetus kicked in time. Connection.

My young children came with me for all the chores. In a carrier pack when they were tiny, or perched on a hay bale in the barn when they could sit. As they grew, they learned to gather eggs and feed the sheep. They stood on milk crates to see into the pens and climbed right in with newborn lambs. But it wasn't always easy. There were times when it seemed everyone needed me at once. Stretched me thin. The spinning wheel stood still.

Moving to the country meant I had little familial support. I began to envy neighbours who had deep connections, parents and grandparents to help. Thomas made swift relationships through his practice and became an integral part of the community, delivering babies, dealing with illness and death, sharing the joys and sorrows of people's lives. I found it a greater challenge to fit in. But never did I want to go back. The farm, the landscape, the sense of endless space all kept me rooted in place.

The first January, there was so much to do. Just keeping the fire going, heating water on the wood stove, and trying to make this wreck into a home consumed me. We did not use the barn. I had enough to do in the house, alone with my dog, no transportation to carry me off. I tore down walls, plastered exposed lath, sanded and painted and made curtains to keep some of the cold away. There were no storm windows other than a few angled fragile frames flapping with dirty plastic. Snow gathered on the sills overnight.

By the following January, we had acquired proper storm windows, some from the neighbour and others from a demolition warehouse close by. The measurements are fairly standard for these old windows, and most of the farmhouses were built to a similar design back in the 1880s. The glass is handcrafted and wobbly. Through many of the panes I can't see the flag on the mailbox, but I wouldn't trade the swirls and bubbles for the contemporary glass that glares and reflects and looks like plastic from a distance. The space between my sashes keeps the weather farther out, where it belongs.

Recently everyone seems to be buying new windows. The sealed double panes that overtook aluminum have a short lifespan, lose their vacuum, and fog up. Vapour condenses and views are obscured. This doesn't happen with the old wooden system. And on a cold January day I find pleasure in the protection of a second window. I feel tucked in.

By our second January, we had a name for the farm. There was a mailbox when we first arrived with Hi Lo roughly painted on it, and though it accurately described the terrain, it didn't really suit us.

With our small flock safely sheltered, we had quarters for our upcoming lambs, and we'd spent a summer weeding out a multitude of lamb's quarters from the gardens. The name *Lambsquarters* seemed to fit.

We had five sheep by then (having bought another from Fred), a few hens, and a marmalade barn cat called Robertson to keep the mice down. Originally set up for a few cows, with loose pens for other stock, the barn had also been used for meat rabbits and was full of filthy, rusting cages. We cleared them out but the cattle stalls remained, as did their hazardous concrete curbs. We established a small pen, built mangers and hay feeders, and cut a sheep door through the rusty metal siding of the stable wall so the flock could come and go. Unless it was storming, I fed their hay outside, carrying a bale and upending it into the square feeder. It was labour intensive, but as sheep only need five pounds per head per day, the work was minimal. Feeling we didn't need to own and house a ram for so few animals, we bought a ram lamb, put him to work, then sent him to the abattoir for our freezer. I don't remember that trip; he was here for a very short time. Shipping animals has been harder since. Is difficult still. But we are meat eaters, meat producers. I cannot defend the practice to vegetarians, but I know my lambs are raised ethically and with great care.

When Blackie aborted a tiny pink fetus early in her gestation, the vet advised selling her. Fred was terribly distressed — he'd have given her another chance — and perhaps I would now as well. But we were neophytes and consulted only the vet who raised fears of contagion and infertility. I should have asked Fred, and from then on, I always did when there was a problem. Since he died, I have often stopped to consider what his advice would be when I have to make a difficult decision.

I had bought an old Vauxhall car by then, Victoria by name, and had my neighbour Harry bolt in seat belts. It was black with red and white leather interior and cost me a pittance. The wheels were tiny and certainly not up to the snowy roads, but when I was observed skidding into the ditch on my way to town one day, two burly neighbours appeared, picked up the car with me in it, and put us back on the road.

Thomas was overwhelmed with his medical practice by then, taking emergency calls one night in three, every third full weekend, and delivering all his patients' babies. His office was open every weekday and Saturdays once a month. As a new and needed young doctor, he attracted most of the neighbours, and as the closest practice to the high school, he helped lots of teens who seemed to feel more comfortable dealing with a young long-haired practitioner who bore no resemblance to either their parents or to the two older conservative physicians in town. Before long, he built up a busy practice of well over 2,500 patients. With roads frequently closed in January and often treacherous, the local doctors worked long hours with little backup. There were no specialists in town, and plenty of accidents with two intersecting highways. I recall one January night when the road was closed, he had to get a snowplough to precede the ambulance to take a patient to a bigger hospital. There were many times before the children were born when I found myself driving for two hours to pick him up in the middle of the night at a tertiary care centre where he had stayed after the ambulance had left, waiting until his patient was settled.

I was still working away room by room to try to make this neglected house into a home. I scraped every single room of the countless layers of wallpaper — much of it painted over in what was likely lead paint. Rooms were dark turquoise, vivid pink, and dirty blue. By that second January, I had redone the living room and the bedroom, and the kitchen functioned. Before we had kitchen cupboards, I hung curtains made from Indian cotton bedspreads from the countertop to hide the mess beneath. We'd retained the tiny electric stove and ancient refrigerator that came with the house, but winter was a good time to plan for their replacement. I spent hours with sketchbook and graph paper, toying with various designs for the kitchen layout.

Garden planning is always a January task. Looking out on the snowy fields and lawns, trekking to the barn in snowshoes, it is a time to dream about spring and planting. The seed catalogues arrived in January then, though now they are in the mailbox earlier and earlier. The local towns offered little in the way of exotica — in seeds or much else. I remember having visitors from the city bring me mayonnaise and Boston lettuce, olive oil and interesting vinegars. Wine from elsewhere. The seeds I would be able to get were solid and reliable, just not very exciting: bantam corn, iceberg lettuce, scarlet runner beans. I sent away for leafy mesclun and mâche, bicoloured corn, petit pois, and slenderette beans. Broccolini and ruby and gold Swiss chard, rainbow carrots and delicata squash.

Flowers didn't particularly intrigue me in those early days. There was just so much to do, and growing food took precedence. There were surviving perennials, and I respected what was there but added little. The backyard was ploughed beside a row of raspberries, with rhubarb and asparagus nearby, so I decided to plant my veggies there, ignoring the shady maple hanging over. I bought a book on organic gardening, which I refer to still. I learned about compost and companion planting. Crop rotation and green manure. Nitrogen, phosphorus, potassium.

When the seed catalogues appeared late in January those first years, during legion snowstorms, arctic temperatures, and conditions too wild even to cross-country ski, I spent hours poring over the pages of lettuces and legumes, carrots and corn. I made lists of what to order, what to plant. I plotted out my patch, recklessly, ignoring that looming backyard maple.

I bought peat pellets and planting soil and made tiny greenhouses with plastic sheets over egg carton planters, a seed of something in each compartment. I planted too much and too soon. The planters warmed on top of the fridge or by the wood stove until seeds sprouted; when I moved them to southern windowsills, they found little sun but lots of freezing breezes.

Many withered on the sill, but what did survive grew leggy and pale, tomatoes unable to keep themselves upright on spaghetti stems. Anaemic lettuce and broccoli. Puny peppers. January gardening is hope gone awry. I've finally learned not to trust it. I still read the catalogues by the fire, and frequently I mark the pages for something new to try — Asparagus peas, Freckles butterhead lettuce, Purple Peacock pole beans. I have visions of future colour and abundance in the garden, currently buried under snow.

※.※

January is a quiet month at Lambsquarters. I catch up on my literary journals, read reviews, and order books from the library, hoping to be first on the list to get a pristine copy. I sit snug by the fire during storms, my collie Flora curled up on a sheepskin mat behind the stove.

Until the barn water freezes.

In the beginning, we watered the stock with buckets, which regularly froze between fillings. I spilt more than one before realizing I could buy heavy rubber pails that heaved with the ice and did not break. To crack through the frozen top, I used a straight iron crowbar, bashing it down into the liquid beneath, learning from experience to stand back to avoid a frozen facial, sometimes flavoured with chicken shit. There is a pipe running from the pump in the house underground to the barn, and I suppose if we had cattle, their warmth would keep it from freezing. But sheep, particularly the five sheep we started with, give off no heat through their thick wool. Snow does not melt on their backs. Our solution was to build and insulate a wooden box around the tap in the barn and to place a light bulb inside to keep it warm enough for water to flow. Mostly it worked, but still it froze in the pails, and I had to carry buckets and buckets, climbing over those old pens and concrete curbs to fill the troughs. I did that for a good eight years before we took on a barn renovation.

By then the house was comfortable. We had insulated and rebuilt the summer kitchen, finding old maple flooring from a demolished house in a nearby town. We extended the stable and made a double garage, the loft above also extended, with gothic gables and windows to the east and west, the north end glassed in. What had been a dark and dirty summer attic became a bright and useful part of the house.

For the barn, our contractor brought in an old guy, Tom McNeil, notorious for smart talking and hard living and famous for his magic in barn shifting. Ours is a bank barn, built into a hill on the north side so loads of hay could be delivered right through the high doors into the mow from the field. The pressure of all the banked earth pushed it south over the years, and the barn was leaning precariously. Old Tom supervised the removal of both south and east walls, attached posts to jacks, and began to winch up the barn. There were chains and pulleys and a lot of home-rolled cigarettes and swearing. The barn, completely open to the wind on two sides, began to crack and grumble as it was heaved up and levelled. "We got her talkin' now!" he said, got in his truck, and drove away for the weekend.

We were left with the barn seemingly floating in the air, wondering if it would hold until the walls were replaced the next week. It survived, despite a storm that felled a tree in the yard overnight. The mortise and tenon beam structure has a magic of its own. We reroofed, refloored, hauled out all the old concrete and metal, and replaced the internal upright thick wooden beams with just four adjustable steel posts. And before the floor was poured, we installed a water system which would give us heated water bowls for each side of the barn, and another for the henhouse off the feed room. No more pails!

But in 2013, in this time of climate upheaval, we had an unusual January weather pattern. Almost no snow, but terribly low temperatures. It stayed below −20°C for days on end, until one day, as I went to do my chores in the morning, the water bowls were steaming and almost empty. All three. Water no longer flowed through the pipes to fill them up. Somewhere the line was frozen solid.

We called the plumbers and they came with all their equipment, all their expertise, but they didn't come quickly as the whole community was frozen. Homeowners in town were told to keep taps running. A restaurant had to close. It was the big freeze.

That year, it turned out to be a problem in the underground pipe from the house. The yards, unprotected by the usual cozy blanket of snow, froze deeper and deeper, and nothing could dislodge the ice. They couldn't help us. For forty-eight days, we carried water to the barn. Forty-eight frigid days of carrying and cursing and wondering why I'd ever chosen this lifestyle.

The next few years, we had enough snow cover to insulate the pipe. We thought we were free, and the inconvenience of having to snowshoe over the yard to get to the barn outweighed the fear of freezing, fear of buckets.

Then suddenly another deep freeze in January 2018, and once again the barn water stopped. The plumbers came (double time on a weekend), worked for a while in punishing temperatures, and determined that, as before, the problem was underground. They left, promising to return with more equipment.

Different plumbers appeared and worked from inside, flooding the basement, racking up hours, tracking debris though the house until ultimately they gave up, promising to return when it was a tad warmer to try to solve it from the barn.

As well as lugging pails to the barn, I now had the basement to clean up, filled with not just water but rust from years of buildup in the pipe. I spent the day running up and down the rickety stairs to wring out my mop until the floor was dry. And then something popped in my knee and I couldn't bend it without pain. Knee swollen, stiff-legged, on snowshoes with a bucket in each mitted hand, I took water to the flock. These are old knees now, old arms, old shoulders. They object.

But they did return, those plumbers — well, not those ones, but others — others we'd have been happy to have seen initially as they rediagnosed the problem and fixed it within an hour. It wasn't underground at all but merely a burned-out heating cable in the insulated box, where all the pipes meet to go to the bowls and the tap. The water ran, the knee improved, and after feigned threats to give it all up, I decided to stay.

※．※

Aging is more obvious for me in January. It is not a happy month, and it ends in another birthday, another reminder that time is waning. I muse on thoughts of leaving for the month another year. But fears of water problems restrict my options. Can I leave someone else to oversee the flock? Would that be fair? Can I keep doing this myself?

I watch my flock; I know them; I detect problems early in my sheep, who disguise any frailty from predators until it cannot be hidden. As prey animals, their instinct is to look strong. Some say there's no such thing as a sick sheep, but that's untrue. I look carefully. I notice. If ears are down, if one is slow to eat, slow to rise, reluctant to respond. I am the shepherd, and Thomas, who equally shares the vision of this life, jokes that he is the hired hand. But I couldn't manage without him. Not now. Not anymore.

There were Januarys when I could, when I had to if he was away, gone with a patient, a delivery, a course, a distant event. I could isolate an ailing ewe and flip her, find a problem in a hoof and sort it with the trimmers. I don't think I'd try to do that now.

Now that I'm in my seventies, I realize I've been catastrophizing for years with each new crisis in the barn, each potential illness in the house. I fear losing my sense of self if I can no longer shepherd my sheep.

Many years ago when I was in my forties, Fred, who had sold me my first ewes twenty years before, telephoned requesting a visit. Over the kitchen table, slowly nursing a cup of tea, he broke down in tears and told me he'd decided to sell his flock. He was in his mid-eighties. A former Mountie, a powerful thinker, and still a big man, he no longer had the stamina required to carry on. I fear that day.

February

In February, the farm begins to stretch. It doesn't fully stir but teases tiny tendrils toward an awakening. Winter still holds fast, the temperatures stay low, the nights long, the ground frozen and white. But in the barn there are subtle signs of change. Greenwood more frequently ventures out from her straw nest, wanders among the ewes, settles on a willing back and gently kneads her paws into the wool. More working animal than pet, she never comes to the house, but she sometimes allows me to hold her on my lap or cradle her and rub her belly.

The ram, however, is getting restless. He throws his weight around, bunting the ewes away from his spot at the feeder, shifting to another slot and bunting again. He rules the courtyard with its heavy hexagonal hay mangers and puts the ewes on notice. He's in charge. They must move. Breeding is over by now — the ewes no longer cycle; he has little to do. Eating consumes him.

We create a new pen, small enough to keep him from backing way up to bunt his way out, large enough to give him comfort. He is annoyed to be kept away from the main flock, though he's only a panel away from the teenaged lambs, his progeny from the year before. They nose each other, chat through the slats, the young ones brave behind the obvious barrier, but he reverses, powerfully pushes his steely skull against the wood, and tries to break through. Between bunts, he rears up on strong hind feet with fluctuating levels of ram ebullience to rest his front hooves on the horizontal boards.

After he splintered the boards and bent a replacement metal gate, we attached heavy two-by-sixes, thick enough to keep him in, strong enough to thwart his cranial karate. He's settled now, focused on food, foregone the fruitless folly of finding cooperative ewes to service. He'll be happier still once his lambs arrive. They will entertain their father, bound and bounce beside his pen.

Left unmolested, the ewes too begin to change behaviour in February. Their gestation is well established, and their hormones shift as their lambs and udders develop. Protective maternal instincts begin to appear, and they jostle against each other for choice places at the feeders. Frequently two ewes will back up, set their large ears behind and high, put their heads down, and crash foreheads a couple of times. It never seems to last for more than one or two bunts, and nothing observable changes from the encounter, but February is when it starts. It alerts me to the coming season, to the time when the fetal lambs spurt with growth and most tax their dams.

The last six weeks of gestation are most critical. Two-thirds of the developing lambs' growth occurs during this time. As the fetuses grow, the ewes' stomachs have less room to break down the hay, so additional concentrated feed is needed. We supplement with oats, which they love, and even though there is lots of bunk space, they constantly vie for a spot at the mangers, sometimes leaving a perfectly good slot to hunt for somewhere better. I am careful to spread the grain evenly unless I have an older ewe I am hoping to fatten up a bit, or those greedy guts I'm trying to restrict. The latter are usually the pushers who devise clever ways to protect their space. They approach diagonally, preventing others from getting in beside them, or stand behind and bunt or shove the others aside. Rather than give up her place, a smaller ewe occasionally ends up piggybacked on her neighbour, gobbling up the grain over the other dam's shoulder.

With the grain, I add powdered molasses. In the early days, I took a cream can to the feed mill in the village, where Martin opened up a tap to fill it. A thick black ribbon of liquid swirled lethargically into the can, and he would cop a taste before turning it off. While it slowly filled, I often sought out Smoky, the mill cat. She had regular litters of kittens and supplied us with barn cats for years. They were used to living rough in the unheated building but were petted by the village children, which kept them from being feral. They made excellent working cats, mousers content to live in the cold and friendly companions during chores.

The molasses is strong stuff. And difficult to manage. I had an old soup ladle in the barn to dish it out, one slow scoop per day into a large bucket of water. I regularly got some on my jeans or my hands, then inside my mitts. And the sheep started sporting sticky muzzles. They loved it though and drank it up. It's important for them to have a high energy content in the feed to prevent ketosis, particularly if they have twins or triplets. Their metabolism gives preference to the fetal lambs; if they don't consume enough sugar, they will break down their own body stores and sicken, even die. The books call it pregnancy disease.

Aging makes many things more difficult for me at the farm, but some practices have improved. I no longer take my heavy old cream can to the mill; it sits under the lilacs, holding sunflower seeds for the birdfeeders. And I no longer waste time with the soup ladle. Molasses, I discovered, doesn't flow any faster in February.

Now I can buy powdered molasses by the bagful. Twenty kilos of sweet-smelling dry feed that perfumes the barn with the essence of brown sugar. Liquid molasses is sprayed on pulverized corn cobs and dried, resulting in a free-flowing delectable confection. I scoop and sprinkle it on their oats. Dessert first.

My scoops are made from cut-away bleach bottles, a trick I learned years ago in that Elysium for grassland sheep farmers, New Zealand. It had been time for Thomas to take a break from his hectic practice, and a time for me to emerge from the jejune routine of caring for two toddlers. We needed change, stimulation, and excitement. Our newlywed neighbours, Maik and Gerrit's son and daughter-in-law, moved onto the farm for six months and took care of our flock, a locum covered the clinic, and we naively set off with an eighteen-month-old and a three-year-old almost halfway around the world.

Those early years on the farm with babies combined elements of pure joy with absolute drudgery. I was alone so much of the time, and it seemed as if laundry and mess ruled my life. Thomas was as busy as he'd ever been. So many nights on call, so many people needing him more than I did. He never had enough time at home, never enough time for patients. I was angry at having to cope alone and frustrated by my isolation on the farm. My patience was tenuous and I felt insignificant. While Thomas needed time and space for himself at home, I craved adult conversation and attention. And help.

To leave it all temporarily took detailed planning. Organizing the farm for a long absence. Finding a locum for the practice. Arranging medical credentials for the Antipodes. Booking flights, arranging short-term medical jobs and places to stay in New Zealand. For the longest lap (of four), I booked an airline seat with a sky bed for my son. It seemed a brilliant idea to have him tucked up in front of me on the bulwark. Unfortunately, he didn't quite fit. Also, the entire area was reserved for mothers, small children, and babies. Few of them content. Thomas got to sit far away with the grownups while I struggled with a tired toddler and an oversized infant in a Procrustean cot.

But it was brilliant when we arrived. Work was well paced so Thomas had shorter clinic days and no hospital call, no obstetrics. Between jobs we travelled, explored, dawdled. I was still the primary caregiver, but I had no farm responsibilities, and it was warm. We left the northern hemisphere in August and arrived to a southern spring. A whole year of spring, summer, spring, summer, spring, summer. No snowsuits, no shovelling, no blizzards. The children and I fed almost every duck in the country. With my son in a pack on my back, my daughter in a cheap folding stroller, we lived a completely different life in various towns. No gearing up for bad weather, no lugging into car seats, just daily strolls to nearby shops, libraries, children's programmes. And ducks.

As well as needing respite from the farm, we were drawn south for the plenitude of sheep. At the time, New Zealand had a population of three million people and over seventy million sheep. I also have relatives there, and I'd been writing to my aunt Dorothy, who warmly welcomed us to her remote sheep station. She was a gentle, hardy widow who strode through her paddocks in a kilt, shepherding her beautiful massive flock of Romneys. Sheep in New Zealand operations are numbered in the thousands or tens of thousands. We were awestruck.

Though I called her my aunt, she was actually my mother's first cousin. They each had a parent who had left England for the colonies, my mother's father to Canada, her mother to New Zealand. Of their descendants, only Aunt Dorothy, her daughter Lorraine, and I chose lives that reflect our heritage in the woollen industry. Our shared relative was a Yorkshire wool broker, and we can identify distant ancestors who were clothiers there as far back as the sixteenth century. They lived on small rural plots with a few sheep, spun and wove their wool into cloth, and sold it in nearby market towns. Aunt Dorothy took that heritage and expanded it to an enterprise that was astounding to me, and would surely have been unimaginable to them.

Her operation was very different from mine. The climate there allows for continuous pasturing, without the need for barns or winter housing. It is all about pasture management and fencing, fertilizing natural grasslands and parasite control.

Probably it's about a lot more than that, but in those days the wool market was strong and the crop exceptional. We arrived at lambing time, with field after field of newborns gambolling among the wild daffodils. Unlike at Lambsquarters, New Zealand has no predators. No wolves, coyotes, foxes. The ewes lamb on the grass, undisturbed by farmers who practise what they call easy care lambing. Instead of our intensive method of checking the barn every couple of hours or so to see if our ewes are in labour, and standing by to help if necessary, the Kiwis leave their flocks to fend for themselves, particularly in the high hill country where separating lambs from their dams or frightening a ewe away from her chosen birthing spot can cause disastrous losses. Shepherds select for productive animals who can deliver and raise their lambs unassisted.

Even with their permanent pasture, New Zealand farmers also supplement at times and need to dish out mixed feed, which they call nuts. In such a remote nation filled with mountainous terrain, they rely on their inventiveness and ingenuity. The bleach-bottle scoop was just one of the ideas we adopted and brought back to our farm.

Because of our antipodal connections, we've been asked to host a group of New Zealand farmers each summer at a gathering after their tour of various large farming operations in our area. They don't come to see our puny little flock, but we join them at a rustic deer-hunting cabin on a back field of a neighbour's oper-ation and serve them local wine or beer. They arrive through the fields by hay wagon, quite a change from the planes and coaches of their cross-Canada tour, and they seem to appreciate getting right out onto the land. Sandaled and sun-damaged, they fre-quently ask about snow: "What kind of snow do you have here . . . is it crunchy snow or wet snow?" So one February, Thomas and

I skied back to this remote area and took a slew of photographs. The snow was piled over the fence in places, almost obliterated the picnic table where many of them sit with their drinks in the July sunshine. The February sky, clear when we set out, filled with mackerel scales, and we were lucky to ski back before the ensuing blizzard. In subsequent summers since, I've been able to show these photos to the visitors from the southern hemisphere who still find it difficult to believe that we deal with so much snow. They wonder how we go out in the winter, if we keep our children inside for the duration, if we are always cold.

We try to explain there isn't just one type of snow. It's a long white season in our Grey County winter, and many factors go into the quality and quantity of the snow we see. It comes in tiny pellets or massive clumps of snowflakes. It's wet and sloppy, dry and sticky, ethereal and lofty. It packs or not. It suits for making angels or for drifting over gates. We do have various names for types of snow: powder, slush, corn — and the always-to-be-avoided yellow snow. And different months tend to produce different sorts, but it all depends on the temperature and humidity, freezing and thawing, sun and cloud.

February is a variable snow month — even more so now with the climate in crisis. I remember it as a winter month in my youth and a difficult time to travel when we first farmed here, the roads thick and icy or closed in blizzards. It was a month of frequent school bus cancellations and closures, and we hunkered down, stormstayed.

Recently we've had plentiful snow. Powder for lovely telemark turns on my skis followed by thick falls of heavy snow and the need for snowshoes to get to the barn. The skiing has been good this February with lots of base and time between storms for the track to settle. Once the trail is in, cross-country skiing is slick and fast with plenty of glide. If it warms too much, the skis ice up and stick, carrying clumps of snow and ice. Then it's not so much skiing as clumsy walking on boards. But waxing my skis gives me back my glide and off I go, sailing along the track through fields and woods.

I am not alone on my trek, but I rarely see my companions. Night creatures mostly, visible only by their own tracks, frequently criss-crossing or shadowing mine. Jumping mice, skunks, flocks of wild turkeys, and red squirrels dance around the fields when I'm out of sight. Deer, fox, and coyote follow my trail.

There is a fox this year, very close. It leaves a single line of tracks alongside the barn, over the road, and into the field across. It's busy at the bottom of the pie-shaped field, tracks weaving in and out of the rail fence into the maple bush. After putting my ski track down, I return to find fox prints within them, following my every turn. At one point, the fox veered off to the right in a bound and left a large fluffy hole in the snow. Back on the track, I picked up its trail again, only this time I found a small tuft of mouse hair, a few frozen red drops of blood on the snow.

A fox can hear a mouse travelling under the snowpack. It can jump far and high in the air and land headfirst, half-buried, tail up in snow to catch a tiny mouse scurrying on the ground beneath. And there is a theory that a fox can precisely pinpoint where that hidden mouse lies by honing in on the Earth's magnetic field. If the fox faces north, its chances of success increase substantially. My fox clearly got its prey.

Snow reveals exactly who we share the land with. A small zig-zag pattern means a skunk, who this year is spending far too much time in the yard, nosing around the base of the birdfeeders, poking into window wells, grubbing near the doghouse. I don't begrudge it the birdseed, but I hope he, or she, doesn't set up housekeeping. I'm careful to shut the shed door each night. I never see the critter, but its nightly visits are evident from tracks.

In the forest, a porcupine nightly waddles in a parenthetical pattern, each dragging foot a bracket in the snow, and the wild turkeys leave large arrowheads in single file, a reminder of their prehistoric past. As the month progresses, different species emerge. Ruffed grouse leave a zipper trail, walking long distances to an open stream to drink, and on warmer days, I see that raccoons are slowly coming out of hibernation, their padded paws leaving handprints in their wake. Deer are constant travellers, fleet of foot, their hoofprints far apart as they sprint through my trail, but I find a shelter where they've bedded down en masse, mattressed with fresh fronds of cedar, scattered with scat. Surrounding hemlocks provide extra warmth as they intercept radiation from snow and nearby vegetation. The deer sleep wisely.

Coyotes also cross my path, though I rarely see them. Large dog-like oblong prints in the snow, a single line if they are moving quickly, alternating if walking, forepaws larger than rear. Whereas I cross the stream on a bridge we call Ponte Vecchio, which Thomas built to replace a derelict structure, the coyote prefers a narrow log. I learn the animals' habits from the trails they leave behind; no doubt they learn from mine.

I noticed a disturbed area on the snow right off the trail one day and skied over to investigate. Thinking it might be a snow dune from wind, I soon realized it was made by a visit from above. A long line of delicate mouse tracks on top of the crust led to a hollow with claw prints and two feathers. An owl must have swooped in for a midnight snack. Each day I discover a new arrival or a return visit. Snow affords the knowledge.

Then a sudden, unseasonable thaw. Within a day, the temperature rises to spring values, and the rain pelts down and down and down some more. The fields are no longer ski runs but small lakes, large ponds, and muddy puddles. Frozen snow paves a treacherous barnyard but within a day it too is gone. Rivers swell, ice dams choke the flow, and towns are evacuated. A small child is fatally swept from his mother's arms.

The climate emergency brings wild weather, great peaks and valleys on temperature graphs. Crops that were once protected by snow cover now rot when a deep freeze follows an unseasonable thaw. We are prone to both flood and drought.

The snow in the woods remains but weakened, wetted, turned into slush. Instead of skis, I need snowshoes to do my daily trek and each footfall lands deep and heavy. Heavier as I age and stiffen. In the early years, we skied at night wearing headlamps if there wasn't moonlight, moving quickly through the still woods, navigating turns and corners with just a small beam of light, various dogs over the years getting in the way or leaving klister on the track: Jessie, her pup Zoë, our friends' yellow lab Jordbær. I learned then to drag my poles on the steep downhills, little plastic rings serving as parachutes to slow me down in the dark. During the days, we set out on open fields behind the barn, racing along on the flat, doing telemark turns down the slopes, spreading powder in an arc. I was never good at this — could only turn to the left — but I loved the exhilarating feeling of speed on my skis, using gravity for nothing but fun, wiping out nearly as often as staying upright, but never an injury.

Now I am cautious. I don't bend as easily, fall as lightly, get back up as quickly, so I avoid the steeper slopes, plough my way through on stiff knees and more frequently rely on dragging those poles, even putting them back between my thighs and sitting on them if things get too scary. I'm still out there, but I'm creaky, wary.

The climate is aging with me, unfortunately, getting cranky in its old age, its warming age, its decline. February thaws were short-lived here in the last century and gave just a few days of temperatures hovering annoyingly around the freezing mark, snow falling as freezing rain or sleet, threatening the power supply, icing the lines, fairying the trees. Then everything settled, the thermometer went back down as it should, and the snow continued. My tracks were obscured, but I was fit enough to set them anew, vary the routes, continue the trek.

February days lengthen, the sun spilling out into long shadows from its southern route, closer each day, warmer, brighter. It's like hard silver on frozen snow in the morning, like molten gold late in the afternoon. The snow varies from deep powder to icy crust. If the sun is strong enough, it sublimates into the granules called corn snow. I ski in bare sleeves, doffing hat and mitts as February wears itself out. Well, I did once.

But currently I'm not as frisky, and February too betrays its historical roots as a snowy month, and again gives up the ghost of winter and nestles into a false spring with rain, with thaw, with slush, with fog, and with mud. You can't ski on mud. You can't ski well on slush. I trade in my skis for slushshoes, as I dub my snowshoes, and traverse the cornfield to the woods. A sudden freeze and there might just be enough snow left to click on the skis, to navigate through the corn stover, the stalks left over after the corn kernels were harvested in the fall. If it's cold enough, with perhaps a smattering of powder, the glide is fantastic and I can speed up without fear or effort. The shallow snow again reveals the wildlife around the farm with tracks of all the nocturnal creatures, and those who hide from detection no matter what the time on the clock.

There is one large central cleared field across the way with forest and streams on each edge. When I was young, I had little concern about exercise and lots of motivation to get myself out in the weather. I was happy to ski well into the night, to start first thing in the morning. Now nights are weary. Mornings are painful.

The barn keeps me moving. Animals must be fed twice a day, bales of hay manoeuvred, pails of grain delivered. But it's all too easy on a cold February day to huddle inside with a book or a journal, to edge my way closer to the fire, to nod off. To eat. Muscles disappear with age; snacks start to show.

This year, my son-in-law challenged me to create a photo essay, to take a picture each day of the same place some distance from the house. He suggested I could send them to him if I liked. This could never have been possible in the early days. Not only did I not need the push, but the technology didn't exist. By the time I took a whole roll of film, had it developed, and put it in the mail, the project would doubtless have dwindled to nothing at all. But now with a camera in my pocket, I can snap the winter tunnel between the trees over the way each day and text it instantly. I cannot cheat; the terrain changes with the weather and the message is dated and timed. The benefit of the journey goes far beyond the physical into the subtle observation of daily change. What new tracks in snow or mud? What other creatures are emerging from hibernation, are edging to the streams to drink, are leaving remains of their midnight kills?

Sometimes creatures come closer. There was a feral kitten on the outer windowsill of the kitchen one cold morning, its back to the pane. On close inspection, it turned out to be avian rather than feline: an eastern screech owl. A fat little bird, feathers puffed, ears pricked, square-shaped, it spent the whole day in view. It shifted around the windowsill for the morning, then hopped down to the verandah and slept, beautifully camouflaged against the unfinished cedar boards sprinkled with snow. I've not seen another.

Another February, I found an unusual and unexpected stowaway creature in my living room. There on the inside windowsill, on a bright snowy morning, was a gray treefrog. While I watched, he flung out his amazingly long tongue and in a trice trapped and swallowed a cluster fly who'd been lazily buzzing around the window. A treefrog in the house? In February? I see them, certainly hear them outside in spring and summer trilling repeatedly in high volume, sounding more like birds than frogs. And I find them camouflaged on fence posts, blending perfectly with grey wood and lichen, or chameleoned to bright green, hiding on foliage. But never before had I seen a frog in the house in the winter.

It soon became clear that my treefrog, Hyla versicolor, had burrowed into a planter I'd had outside all summer, intending to spend the winter there on top of my potting table under the lilacs. It chose a cozy hibernaculum in with my Christmas cacti, three small pots inside an earthenware planter, and was likely surprised to wake up inside a heated human house.

The gray treefrog usually hibernates under leaves or debris on the forest floor. Quite astonishingly, it is able to survive sub-zero temperatures by producing a kind of antifreeze for its system, allowing its heart and lungs to pause functioning until temperatures rise and rewarm it. My guy couldn't have frozen: I had brought the plants inside before frost, but still it must have slept through until that day. With the ground frozen outside, evicting him wasn't an option; all I could do was try to keep him alive until spring thaw.

For once, I was thankful for all the cluster flies in the house. Annoying pests, they buzz around reading lights at night, bang into lampshades, ping off the pressed-tin kitchen ceiling. When not airborne, they assume a torpid state in winter and are easily caught, either napping in a cluster in the corner of a window or dawdling around the pane. I began to collect them, one at a time, and put them within striking range of the frog. Instantly, it snapped out its lethal tongue and devoured the fly. The tongue seemed to be as long as the frog itself. Not only is the frog incredibly accurate with each strike, but a sticky mucus on the tongue helps trap the accosted fly.

I felt a new responsibility. Not only did I have a barn full of animals to tend, but now an amphibian had moved in and demanded refuge. The first thing I did, after feeding it, was to succumb uncritically to anthropomorphism and arrogantly give it a gender and a name. Louis the Grenouille.

Louis began to divide his time between the pot and the windowsill, and I fed him whenever I saw him out. I provided a small container of water. He had no interest in dead flies, so despite the plethora of corpses after a sunny day, I continued to gather up live specimens for his pleasure.

It isn't that easy to warm up to a cold-blooded creature, but I've always been fond of treefrogs, and I'm a sucker for most critters. Louis became a part of the menagerie, a welcome presence when he appeared on the sill, decorative, low-care, unique. He seemed to survive easily on just a few flies a day, so I let him stay, at least until spring.

March

March roared in like a rampant lion, gusting and chilly, and with luck it will go out as docile as the first new baby lamb. The ram was released on November 5 last year, and his eagerness matched that of Guy Fawkes, exploding exuberantly from his pen to the waiting ewes, some shy, some disdainful, some anxious for the meet and greet. The first birth is due on March 31, and ewes are remarkably accommodating at delivering on time. But at the beginning of the month, our concentration is on shearing.

To prepare, we carefully watch the weather forecast to be certain the flock will be dry. On clear days, we continue to feed them outside, but if there's the slightest chance of precipitation, we close them into the stable. The yearlings, who have been kept away from the ram during breeding, are returned to the ewes, now crowding the pen with their growth. Our fleeces can be as much as eight inches in length, so each sheep expands wool-wise as well as pregnant-belly-wise over the winter, taking up increasing amounts of space. We try not to squish them, as we strive to find the perfect balance of indoors and out to keep them both dry and content.

For a number of years, we've had a world-class sheep shearer, a man who blindfolded with a black cloth can shear a sheep in record time. Part of our preparation for him is of the stable itself; a large area must be cleaned out to set up the shearing board, and another large space for the sorting table. We also organize gates and pens to make the process run smoothly. On shearing day, the flock is sequestered in a holding pen, with extra hurdles in place to decrease its size as the animals are moved. The more they are crushed, the calmer they will be.

Shearers are notoriously busy, notoriously independent. It can be difficult to have them commit to a date, a time. One March, a few days before he was expected, I got a call that the shearer was nearby and ready. He'd be here shortly. Thomas was out of town; I had no one else to help; it was storming. In haste, I tried to organize the barn. We have an old pig scale we use to weigh lambs — a big heavy metal cage on wheels — and it was right in the way. I had a terrible time trying to heave it and realized too late that it had frozen to the floor. In a final herculean effort, I pulled it loose. It didn't just release from the floor but toppled toward me, pushed me down, landed on top of me.

When I freed myself, I realized immediately that my arm was broken. My March break. I scrambled outside, took off my ring and my watch, plunged my arm in the snow. It was crooked. Heading west.

Everything was complicated by the storm. I'd left my car at the road so the neighbour could blow the snow from the lane, but now I needed him to drive me to the hospital. He came immediately, as he always did, Gerrit, my flying Dutchman, and drove me carefully and uncharacteristically slowly in his 4x4 through the storm to town. I believe I was swearing rather immoderately. He stayed calm.

In those days, we knew everyone at the hospital. The doctors, the nurses, the patients. It was the place Thomas had spent his time as a young physician, where I frequently visited and waited for him, where our young children accompanied him on weekend rounds, played in the paediatric playroom, wheeled themselves around in kid-sized wheelchairs. My flying Dutchman would have stayed, but I released him home knowing I'd be looked after, recognized, patched up. He carried on and blew the lane, moved my car, made things ready for the shearer, who did arrive, bringing helpers with him. I had no part of the shearing that year. I spent the rest of the afternoon high on morphine while the doctor on call, Thomas's colleague and our friend Hugh, dealt with much more serious injuries from car crashes and organized ambulance transfers in the storm. When my X-rays came back, he announced with some glee that I would be able to eat, as I wouldn't need surgery. He is a man who likes his food! Eating was pretty much the last thing on my mind that day. He determined that my arm would never be quite straight, but it would function. It does. If a little to the west.

We give ourselves more time to organize now and have more help. Our daughter arrives with her partner and our two grandsons who each have a role. When he arrives, our shearer Donny finds us ready to go — all set up, just waiting for him to attach his gear to a hook on a ceiling beam, plug in his motor, change his boots for shearing moccasins, his jacket for a shearing singlet, attach his comb to the handpiece, and oil his cutters.

While the shearer is setting up, Thomas and our son-in-law lead the animals out, a few at a time, to the gangway, where they are further contained. Then one by one, they are handed off to the shearer. My daughter and one grandson operate the gates, and the other keeps the shearing board clean and helps me deal with the fleeces. It all happens at blizzard speed, the wool peeling off in one beautiful carpet of fleece, the belly wool discarded but the rest intact. Donny scoops the bundle in his arms and throws it in a cascading arc onto the slatted sorting table, cut side down. The table, about four by eight feet, is constructed from wooden strips with inch-wide spaces, allowing any second cuts to fall through. A second cut occasionally occurs if the shearer goes over an area twice, cutting a short bit of fleece. These bits are useless for the spinner. Woollen dross. Luckily, Don is a gun shearer (as the best are called) and rarely overlaps his shearing comb, so there are few. In my attempt to keep up with his lightning speed, I hastily skirt the edges of the fleece, discard soiled and matted bits, turn the sides to the middle, and roll the fleece into a fluffy ball from tail to tip cut side up, revealing the luxurious shiny white wool that's been protected from the elements all year. I mark each precious parcel with the name and number of the animal and line them up individually on a tarp on the floor, then scurry back for the next delivery.

Removing the year's growth of wool is the big reveal. Not only do we discover the quality of each fleece as the shears expose the undergarments of wool to the light, but the ewes in their dishabille display all their fecund glory.

The shorn ewes pink up, their skin sports a healthy blush beneath the fine snowy film of remaining wool. When they are all quite naked, we move on to the black ewes, which are harder to shear because it is much more difficult to see where the wool ends and the pelt begins. A man who can shear blindfolded has an advantage with black sheep. He shears them clean.

Black fleece absorbs rather than reflects light, so knitters and weavers also find dark wool more challenging. But it is also more desirable, as it is both rich in hue and sleek with lustre. It is lovely to blend, and the greyer fleeces make beautiful heather tones when dyed. I can ask a much higher price for my coloured wool. It is more valuable for both its rarity and its clarity.

We say every year that the last animal finished is the one we've been looking for all day. An entire year's growth is off in a trice, and it takes me longer to bag and tag it, readying it to sell to handspinners, than it has taken our man to shear it.

The following day, I place each fleece in a clear plastic bag, write the animal's name and number and the price on the tag, and take them up to the mow, where Thomas has now moved the sorting table. I pile them on, two to a trip up the stairs, and cover the lot with the tarp until the buyers begin to arrive. It makes a full day.

Purebred livestock are identified by flock or herd letters, a number, and a year letter. When we applied for our flock letters, Thomas had the brilliant idea of *ewe and ram*, which would spell EAR when tattooed in their ears. Unfortunately, someone else beat him to this ridiculous joke and these letters were unavailable. Our next choice, TAB, suffices, designating the flock as *Thomas and Barbara*. The year letters go in the opposite ear along with the number, which we assign at birth. Because our wool clients ask details about our sheep, we name our lambs starting with the first letter of the flock year. When the year was E, we were able to name three ewe lambs after our grandmothers: Ethel, Elsie, and Euphemia.

Ear tags, which we also use, are particularly helpful after shearing when the sheep all look different without their prelapsarian wool. They too notice the difference and respond with much sniffing and snuffling, some bunting and some confusion. Suddenly there is lots of space in the pen and no more crowding at the feeders. But a newly slimmed sheep can find fresh mischief.

The day after shearing, when I am doing the chores, I hear a loud and repeated bleating. Because I lost the hearing in my right ear half a lifetime ago, I'm unable to locate where sound originates. You need two functioning ears for that. An autoimmune condition caused the deafness and it can't be treated, so I've been stuck for years with the annoying affliction. I stand in the gangway getting more and more frustrated as I try to figure out which animal is making so much noise and why. No one seems in distress, and no one seems to be opening her mouth to baa. But the pen is in two parts, with the water bowl encaged in the middle, so it's impossible to watch everyone at once. I look to one side — no visual baaing, but sound. I look to the other side — same story. Finally I enter the pen and begin counting, hoping to figure out if anyone is missing. It seems unlikely. The rest of the stable is very clean, which it wouldn't be if a sheep were rampaging on the loose. The water bowl area is empty — no sheep hiding there.

I start by counting the black sheep, and initially the count seems correct. Counting sheep is rather different for the shepherd from the cartoon version. They rarely stand still for my convenience, particularly just after shearing when they seem wary of what might be coming next. Eventually I realize that the count is off: one of the ewe lambs (who had a habit of getting her head caught in the feeder until it got too big) is missing. For some minutes, I stand there flummoxed. No way can I locate the sound, so I just have to figure it out. Eventually, the only possibility seems to be a new feeder that is up against the stone wall. There's a small concrete retaining ledge at the bottom, and somehow she must have climbed up on it, wedged her way along for a tasty bit of hay in behind, and carried on until she was down off the ledge and wedged underneath the feeder itself.

Sheep generally do not have the gift of reverse. Of course they can back up, but it rarely occurs to them if they find themselves caught. I haven't counted the times I've had to release an animal who has stuck her head through the rungs of a rail fence, grazed along the length of it only to find that the space between the rails is much thinner there than where she went in. She'll pull and pull trying to get out but doesn't think to back up to where she started. She calls; I assist.

After I detach the feeder from the wall, she eventually bounds out. I take a length of log we keep for such an event (lambs can be excellent escape artists) and plug the hole where she went in. If I don't, I'm quite sure she'll go right back as soon as I leave. I don't dub the yearlings *teenagers* for nothing.

༄༅

March 8 is International Women's Day, and this year it occurs the day after shearing. It's a day when I reflect on many things, not least on women in agriculture. When we first bought Lambsquarters, farm wives had few property rights. Despite their contribution to agriculture, if they left their marriage, they were not necessarily entitled to a share of the property. Just days before we obtained the title of our farm in 1973, the Supreme Court of Canada ruled against a woman who claimed her share of the family ranch after the couple had separated. It was not considered relevant to the case at the time, but surely it is not insignificant that she was assaulted by her spouse before the separation, hospitalized with a broken jaw. The court determined that because she had not significantly contributed financially to the initial acquisition of the ranch and because her name was not on the title of the property, she had no claim to a financial interest in the operation after their separation.

Despite the fact that this woman had spent twenty-five years not only contributing to the physical work of the farm — swathing and raking hay; driving teams of horses, trucks, and tractors; treating, branding, and dehorning cattle — she also ran the ranch by herself for months every year while her spouse was away working off the farm. It seems likely she also ran the kitchen, the laundry, the child care, the acquisition of supplies. She lost her case at the provincial level on the basis that she had not contributed cash to the operation, and the court accepted her spouse's argument that she just did what any rancher's wife did, which he agreed was basically everything.

The case was subsequently heard by the Supreme Court with the same outcome. The judges were all men. An overwhelming outcry among women across the country eventually led to equal property rights in Canada. It was not enshrined in the Charter of Rights and Freedoms until 1982, coincidentally a full hundred years after the British Married Women's Property Act of 1882, which for the first time had allowed married women to own property of their own. Until then, a woman's possessions and acquisitions were relinquished to her husband upon marriage.

So when we came to Lambsquarters, if I had not had my name on the title, I'd have had no claim to the property if I had decided farming wasn't for me. My name is on the title, although an element of sexism remains as it follows Thomas's name, despite the fact that both my first and last names come before his alphabetically. He is listed by his profession; I am dubbed "Married Woman." Not exactly the identity I aspired to or recognized.

Much has changed since those days. No longer do farm-to-farm salesmen ask for "the boss" when I answer the door. My stock answer was to reply, "You're looking at her." Keeping my own name was such a novelty in those early years that Gerrit, hearing horrified gossip in the village that we might not actually be married, vouched for us saying he'd seen our wedding pictures. He hadn't.

None of this matters now, and women in agriculture are increasingly recognized for the work they do in all aspects of agricultural business, education, administration, and on-farm labour. The veterinary college down the road has shifted from all men to almost all women, and most of the local large animal vets we see at the farm are women. I hear complaints from some farmers about all these women taking over the vet school, not that the veterinarians are incompetent or incapable of dealing with large animals, but there is some principle that offends them. Occasionally we see evidence that these women are underestimated and have had to assert themselves; Thomas once innocently attempted to guide a vet's truck into the barnyard and was instructed rather forcefully that she knew how to drive. And of course she did (which he never doubted), reversing the big 4x4 easily in the tight space between the stone wall and the wooden gate. She quickly and competently went on to deliver two live lambs by Caesarean section.

This is one of the advantages of aging on the farm. Despite my experience of gender discrimination, I've witnessed a huge improvement in the way women are treated and accepted in all aspects of farming. And gone are the days when a neighbour must find her way to our front door and ask to be protected from her abusive husband. Unfortunately, abuse still exists, but instead of just providing protection and transportation, I can now support women's shelters, helplines, volunteer drivers, and crisis intervention. And I wouldn't now stay silent. It's better than it was.

※.※

Many farms on our road were handed down through descendants of the same families who colonized the land a couple of centuries ago, bestowed — as if it were theirs to give — by the Crown. Our home on native land.

This is the traditional territory of the Iroquois Confederacy: the Mohawk, Oneida, Onondaga, Cayuga, Seneca, and Tuscarora Nations known as the Haudenosaunee, of the Ojibwe/Chippewa and Anishinaabe.

In 1836, 1.5 million acres of this area's fertile farmland were acquired by the British Crown under the Saugeen Tract Purchase, known as Treaty 45 ½. As a consequence, the First Nations Peoples were displaced to settlements farther north, disrupting a sacred connection to the area that goes back many thousands of years. A tragic part of our colonial history, our imposition of foreign values on the first inhabitants of this land.

Through generations of settler families, the farms carved from these Indigenous grounds frequently fell into the calloused working hands of the youngest son, not the eldest through primogeniture. Here it seemed to be the one who held on longest, who was still living at home when his parents retired and moved to the village. Daughters-in-law changed their names, moved in, pasted new wallpaper, updated the paint, and bore more sons to keep it all going. Their daughters grew up and moved up or down the road, taking on the neighbour's name, providing sons and daughters of their own.

Our road was called Concession 2, or colloquially "the 2nd." I learned from *The Canadian Encyclopedia* that:

"Concession line" is principally an Ontario term for the straight country roads, parallel to one another,

upon which farm lots face. They are complemented
by perpendicular side roads, which together create
a gridwork that covers each respective township.
Each rectangle of roads commonly embraces 10
farm lots of 100 acres (40.5 ha) in size. During the
19th-century era of initial settlement in Ontario,
these lots were conceded (hence "concession") by
the Crown to individual applicants seeking title in
exchange for raising a house, performing roadwork
and land clearance, and money.

There is no mention of First Nations' lands or treaty rights or
Indigenous Peoples, who most certainly lost the land to arbitrary
divisions and benefactions.

Concession suggests a sense of reluctant agreement or admitting
defeat. And also of generosity of farmers who made concessions to
neighbours, to the community, and to the greater good by donating
land for schools, churches, graveyards. In the early days, farmers
would not have survived or thrived without the help of their neighbours. Barns were raised in bees. Equipment and labour were shared.

During our time here, the 2nd has changed from a dusty
gravel road to a paved thoroughfare. More traffic zips along now
at higher speeds, and more houses have been built on small acre-
ages carved off the original hundreds. Fewer farmers live on the
road, and each year another century-farm family seems to disappear, the land swallowed up by bigger operations.

At the millennium, to cut costs, the provincial government
amalgamated townships, which necessitated road name changes.

Some concessions became county roads; others disappeared into an unintelligible numerical system. Concession roads that were originally numbered sequentially by twos now jump from 14 to 9 to 22. Sideroads that followed a progression of fives went from 5, 10, 15, 20 to 41, 47, 49, 23. If there's a pattern, it continues to mystify me. In the old system, I could always figure out where I was from the road signs; now I'm confused. If I'm lost, I'm lost; the signs won't guide me.

But the greater loss is the community itself. It's no longer possible to support a family on a hundred acres. And smaller families find fewer heirs to stay on the farm. Much of the bucolic image I had of historical farms turns out to be false as many of my neighbours grew up in serious poverty and deprivation, without the conveniences of the city. Power and plumbing came late.

As farms got bigger and bigger, their owners made their own land amalgamations, and superfluous wooden bank barns began to fall into ruin. They say you need animals to keep a barn healthy, perhaps only because you must attend daily. If the roof leaks, you perceive the need to fix it. If some siding blows off, you'll protect your hard-earned hay and straw from spoiling. If it's empty, it's soon derelict.

Houses too suffer. In the past few years, I've counted nine farmhouses on the road that have disappeared, a tenth at risk. Some were beyond repair, some of poor original quality, some were expropriated by government projects, and some, I suspect, were just not modern enough to suit their new owners. Beautiful yellow brick houses — bigger, newer, and grander than mine — have been demolished, their hand-hewn frames and square iron nails reduced to rubble, replaced by pretend stone and plastic siding. Inviting farm kitchens with comfy chesterfields and wooden tables are replaced with chipboard and artificial granite islands and flat-pack fixings.

My neighbour to the south died and the farm was sold. It had not been a happy house, but nevertheless I felt the loss when a bulldozer knocked the place down and buried it all in a few short hours. Now that little evening kitchen light over the way is gone and the yard is a cornfield. As so often happens in disturbed ground, hundreds of poppies bloomed later in the summer. I snapped off pods and saved them to plant here at Lambsquarters. A small reminder of my former neighbour, who more than once needed our help before she was able to leave her difficult situation.

And once again, I recognize my increasing age. The complaints that come with my reluctance to accept change. My nostalgia for a time before modern conveniences, when women rocked on their front porches shelling peas to the sounds of bees and cicadas, their children playing at their feet, everyone content. Perhaps that *did* happen on the odd summer afternoon, but more likely the women were sweating over wood-burning cookstoves, trying desperately to feed their families on what they could grow, or buy with the egg money. Copper boilers make beautiful planters; I'm glad I don't have to use one for laundry. And few of us would choose to revisit winter privies.

Fallen barns are particularly sad to see. The siding goes first, its outer layer revealing all the leftovers of its previous life. The mouldy hay in the loft, the dusty straw. Piles of rotted manure mounding the stables. Eavestroughs fall off and water seeps down to the foundation. Huge stone boulders, placed by hand and horsepower over a hundred and a half years ago, loosen from their mortar and open huge cracks. And then the corners crumble. Roofing materials flip up in storms and are not tacked down. Whole sheets fly off, and it won't be long before all that's left is the frame of adzed tree trunks, once painstakingly fitted by mortise and tenon, holding themselves upright for a few more years, kept there by some magic of engineering and architecture known intuitively or inherited by the original builders.

Farming has outlived the need for the high bank barn, built into the side of a hill (or hilled up) to facilitate delivering hay into the mow — originally loose on a wagon, then in small square bales, to be piled to the top beams. Few farmers even own small balers now, and they routinely ensile their hay in huge round or square bales wrapped in plastic and lined up in barnyards or against fencerows. There are coverall barns with plastic roofs, and pole barns all laid out on one level. No need for ladders on the inner sides of the mow to climb up and throw bales down by hand; they are now picked up by the priapic attachments to front-end loaders, and tractors deposit them in large round feeders or chop them in a total mixed ration machine. Hauled behind a tractor, or incorporated into the bed of a truck, a TMR is a large mixing bowl of a machine, a massive food processor that mechanically combines large quantities of forage with a balanced measure of fodder, grains, and supplements. In large operations, it is driven right down a barn passageway, the contents equally spread from a delivery chute at one side for the livestock on the other side of a feeder fence. Hands off.

From horses to open tractors to bale throwers to plastic. Everything changing, squeezing more from each acre, feeding more mouths, using more science, improving production. The removal of fencerow trees and vegetation to create larger fields and the increase in pesticide use have devastated insect, avian, and animal populations, threatened the wildlife corridors. Every agricultural improvement has its cost to the environment.

There was a time not so many years ago when new barns were still being built in the old way, particularly after a disaster. But the last one I can remember was such a novelty that the elementary school children were taken from their classes to watch the raising. Something they'll never likely see again. So many men climbing up the beams, hammering on the roof, putting on the pine siding, and as many women setting up tables in the farmyard to feed the workers. Bringing sandwiches and lemonade. And pies.

We still see the odd barn being restored with new wood siding, a shiny metal roof, a reinforced foundation, but it's rare. Our own barn is carefully checked for failure, the beams tested for soundness, the roofing nails repounded, the wiring replaced where it's worn. It's an unusual structure as it was built with recycled timbers a hundred years ago after the original barn was struck by lightning and burned to the ground. There are empty mortises on the uprights where previous tenons lived. And I've no way of knowing the provenance of these logs. Another structure's loss was our gain. We've put a lot of work into maintaining our barn. A new roof, new siding, windows, doors, a poured concrete floor and yard, and a watering system. And as long as we can persuade our neighbours to make small bales of hay for us, we will continue with our antiquated system, antiquated as we now are. But we've been warned that if the baler breaks, it will be neither repaired nor replaced.

茶.架

Long before dawn, I wake to the vision of lights flashing on the ceiling above the bed. Occasionally, if there's an early vehicle coming from the east, there is a fleeting flash of light, and a snow-plough will cast blue flickers. But there is nothing to see out the east window and the lights continue in their unique pattern. I sit right up and look to the north, where off in the distance there's a tiny visible stretch of the old 2nd. To my horror, there is a fleet of flashing lights — mostly red now — and over the trees an ominous orange glare. Fire.

Thomas suggests we walk across the fields to identify what is burning and try to help. He feels our truck might impede emergency traffic. Because of the forest between farms, we can't identify the source of the fire. The moon is down and the night is pitch. We stumble across our hayfield with a flashlight, down through the pie-shaped field, over the line fence into the neighbour's, and still we are unsure. It isn't the closest barn or the house, but it could still be the neighbour's house up the hill. Not until we are quite close can we discern that it is a barn. A beautiful well-cared-for barn, flaming beyond control.

So many emotions. Knowing this is not an active barn, that there are no animals, no livestock inside, is hugely comforting. Watching the demise of a handcrafted wooden bank barn is devastating. And yet it is startlingly — guiltily — beautiful. The sharp contrast of florid fire colours against the thick blackness of the sky; the outline of the barn-shaped beams as the siding melts away, the sheer power of the conflagration, undulating and swaying, licking through the ridge pole, showering sparks into the wind, exploding rubber tires and tanks of gasoline in earth-shaking tremors. The sounds. The booms and crackles, the whooshing and purring. The absolute force. A terrible beauty.

We stand shivering in the field with our neighbours, our friends. The parents, their grown children, their nephews, their brother. All in the field in front of the barn watching it burn, blessing the east wind, that beast, finally doing some good in blowing the sparks away from the house, from other structures or danger. We stand helpless, watching the fire, watching the firefighters in their Michelin Man suits standing between the burning barn and the house. Equally helpless as all they can do, as the ironic expression goes, is save yet another ruined stone foundation, the only thing that won't burn. For there is no safe way to tackle a barn fire. It is just too big, too combustible, too dangerous. They are carefully watching the track of the flames, checking that power lines do not relay sparks to the house, making sure the land behind is safe. Their trucks line the roadside, and more arrive from another community. A two-alarm fire.

John, our next-door neighbour, son of Gerrit the Flying Dutchman and Maik, saw the sparks first and alerted the fire department and the residents. He ran over and helped remove equipment before the flames engulfed, likely taking more of a risk than he should have. The young couple living in the house are stoic, clearly sad, but thankful no one is hurt, no livestock succumbed. They are to be married shortly and intended to take photos at the barn. I weakly offer ours.

We stand and remember stories about old Tom Davis, who lived there with his sister Isabel for as long as any of us can remember. They kept some cows, some pigs, and quite a few empty cigarette packages and aluminum pie plates in the barn in later days. He drove an old blue truck until he had a crash on the corner of the 2nd. When he was a kid, John used to cut the grass and do Tom's storm windows, and he reminisces about getting paid once a year. "Payday, payday," Tom would say and reach into his pocket for a bill. Sometimes it would be a fifty, but the odd year Tom's eyesight mistook the colours and John got a two-dollar bill for his efforts. He laughs about it standing there in the cold wind.

Eventually the frame collapses, and the old stores of hay and straw fall flaming to the stable floor, where nothing has been fed or bedded for so long and now never will again. We start to disperse, heading home, everyone else in trucks and Thomas and I heading back along the road to shiver our way back, climb the fence into our forest to follow our snow-covered corduroy road to knock-down corner, to climb up the hill and take the chute back to our own barnyard. Our own precious old wooden bank barn, filled with pregnant ewes, shorn now and shut in against the cold, helpless and dependent. To farm is to be implicated. To make concessions.

Back in the barn a few days after shearing, it's time to treat the flock medically. Every year, we give a booster vaccination for clostridial diseases and a topical treatment for parasites. As if they haven't been bothered enough, we arrive again with those crushing hurdles and pile them all into a small space. Thomas is a whiz with the needle, and my job is to fill the syringes and hand them to him, a jab at a time. Each year I amuse myself by rereading the names of the conditions we are attempting to prevent including blackleg, black disease, and pulpy kidney, but there's no pleasure in experiencing these conditions, so we never miss the chance at prevention. Just after shearing is the ideal time. It's easy to administer a subcutaneous injection when the skin is so readily available. Thomas pulls up a fold, inserts the needle, pushes the plunger, makes a mark on the treated sheep with a special crayon stick, and moves on to the next. They were a tad jumpy this year, and I determine to buy some steel-toed boots. Big Stella, extra heavy with a number of lambs on board, found my foot a comfortable place to stand and was quite reluctant to move. Farming equals bruising.

The topical treatment is much easier. I use a large syringe, no needle, and fill it with the right dosage for each animal — more for the ewes than the lambs. It is an orangey oily liquid and initially shows up on their backs after I've squirted them, so there's no need to use the marking crayon. The black ewes are harder to see, but the liquid gleams if I look on an angle, so I'm quickly finished. We see no evidence of critters, but it's possible that lice can be brought in on the shearer's equipment, so we treat prophylactically. Now, and again in a fortnight's time in case there might be eggs yet to hatch.

These jobs completed, the flock is left to enjoy their new freedom from wool and concentrate on their food and their fecundity. Soon we'll be back bothering them at all hours, looking for signs of labour. But for now, they have a couple of weeks' peace. As do we.

March is often fickle, but drastically changing weather patterns have made it capricious, mad, even evil, shape-shifting from winter to spring, spring to winter, blowing a vortex around the farm from one day to the next. Blustering to begin, it settles after the first few days, calms; brightened, lengthened days pull heat from the sky, melting snow melting ice. It is a wonder to walk the gardens, see the tips of daffs, tulips, scilla poking through bare ground, surrounded by leaves left over from fall's fallings. As the skies throw back their winter clouds, they emerge bluebird blue and the sun feels warm. Almost hot. Until it stops.

Suddenly the winds, March winds, tear in from the east, from the north, gusting fiercely from the west and picking up great moisture from the lakes. Our high ground reaches up like a giant hand to stop them, only to have the snow pause, consider, and then fall in drifts, in banks, in rough carpets over the bareish fields, the greening lawns, the cornstalks. All is covered, bitter, so much worse for the promise broken. Robins turn tail, the few who had ventured. Red-winged blackbirds stop trilling that first welcome quavering gurgle, hunch their red epaulettes, and sidle off. Only the tundra swans keep coming. Their long white necks like ribbons in the streamers of snow, their landed bodies lumped in tracts of open water like ice jams, floating together toward their own disappearance. Like the ice, they won't stay forever, but continue north when the melt finally comes to stay.

By March, it seems winter will never end. Waiting for spring is more difficult for me as I age. My joints hurt more; my muscles are stiff and cramp at will. Just by pointing my toe into my barn boot, I'll spend the next minutes trying to walk it out before I need to climb the hay mow. I have a trigger finger that locks in the off position tight against my palm and won't go back by itself. I have to take off my mitts and snap it back with the other hand. Creepy. My shoulders hurt, and I tire easily. I want it to be warm, to be bright. On the worst days, it seems as bad as January, when there is no hope for improvement. On the best days, it is a tease. Beware more than the ides of March. The whole month can't be trusted.

During the thaw, Thomas heads down to the bush with his equipment: drill, clippers, hatchet, saw. The old bus house, once at the roadside to shelter waiting school-aged children, now punctuates the sugar bush, storing the buckets, lids and spiles, the iron kettle, the sieves and ladles — the trappings of the ancient craft of sugaring off. Maple syrup has been made for centuries, originally by the First Nations of the Eastern Woodlands, such as the Abenaki, Haudenosaunee, and Mi'kmaq, who taught the settlers. Sap is a natural product, dripping freely from the trees on sunny days; one need only collect and boil it down to make a delicious sweet confection.

Most years, Thomas needs snowshoes to tramp through the bush on those first days above freezing when the sun hits the trees' crowns, but this year the snow is a memory and the forest floor is bare. Each tree is drilled, often more than once depending on its girth; the metal spiles gently set in. Tall narrow metal buckets hang from a hook on each spile, or tap, their lids hinged. The first day, the sap runs strong — not a drip-dripping into the pail, but a steady stream as if the trees had been holding their breath, or crossing their legs, just waiting to be tapped.

When the nighttime temperatures are low, negative pressure draws moisture from the roots of the maples up through the trunk. If the sun warms up the next day, the water-logged tree will happily give up its overflow of sap. Ideal temperatures are in the range from −5°C overnight to +5°C the following day. Continual tapping is not harmful. As long as the tap does not pierce the heart of the trunk, the tree will not be hurt. Heartwood is deeper than the reach of the spiles, so the trees suffer no loss with our gain.

The commercial producers use blue plastic tubing instead of buckets. It wends its way through the bush like a maze of translucent handrails, staying in place throughout the year. Gravity helps with the flow through the tubes, but most large producers also use sap extractors and vacuum pumps to draw the sap from the trees. Large shallow rectangular pans on stainless steel evaporators encourage the water in the heated sap to vaporize and reduce the liquid to syrup. Reverse osmosis can speed up the process by extracting pure water from the sap before it reaches the evaporator, but boiling is central to the production and must be completed before the syrup is ready for its pancakes, waffles, ice cream, or to flavour ricotta for sfogliatelle.

Massive oil-burning structures operate in grand laboratory-like conditions. The syrup from these commercial operations is marketed in containers decorated with snowy woodland scenes of log sugar shacks, small children carrying sap buckets, and horse-drawn wagons with wooden barrels of sap, but these bucolic images, including their open fires and iron kettles, rarely reflect the process.

Except for here at Lambsquarters, and no doubt in plenty of other small farms that use the hiatus between winter and spring to work on bush hygiene and create something sweet and wonderful from the deadfall and tangle of winter blowdowns and firewood offcuts. From year to year, Thomas replenishes his stack of fuel with the detritus of maple trees past whose final generous task is to burn in an open pit under an old iron sap kettle. The kettle was a gift years ago, and though it was missing a handle on one side, Thomas has kitted it up with a cradle of chains to make it hang level over the fire.

Each year, he shovels snow from the firepit, hauls away last year's ashes, and starts a new fire, calling it into the fire department in case the smoke is reported, and he settles into the hard labour of hauling dead trees and huge branches from his stash, lugging logs too old or punky for inside, and creating the glowing coals that will heat the kettle and set the sap to boil. On a good day, it can be a chore to keep up with the running sap, but on a slow day, it's a danger to burn the fire so hot that the sap evaporates too much. It's more of a sense than a science, and over the years, his senses have sharpened. If once it boiled dry, it would never happen again. If it boiled furiously enough to overflow and drown the fire, it wouldn't get that full again.

It takes a lot of energy, patience, and commitment to do this work. I like to send Thomas off with a good breakfast because there's every chance he'll not return for lunch. With the hens laying well in the lengthening days, I prepare fresh eggs in various ways: poached on homemade whole wheat toast, fried with potatoes from the root cellar, even boiled with toast soldiers. But to set him up best, I bake hot cross buns to split for French toast, dip them in egg, sauté in butter, and serve with the very first batch of syrup.

Maple sap from the tree is 98 percent water, so there is just a tiny taste of sweetness to begin. Of course, water is central to the syrup, but it must be boiled down in a ratio of forty to one. So forty buckets of sap for one of syrup. And each bucket is hand-carried, often from quite a distance from the fire. Over the previous summer, undergrowth obscured the paths into the forest, and depending on the snow cover, the trips to gather buckets can be tricky. Most years, the first pass on snowshoes sets the trail, but a thaw will freeze the packed areas into mini skating rinks. Small sticks that brush your thighs to begin will poke you in the eye if lots of snow melts, and buckets that initially had to be lifted up will need to be reached down as the ground lowers with the thaw.

This year, the snow melted before it all began, then patchily returned. There's a crunch in each step, but the taps are still at optimum height, drilled anew in a different spot each year. The warm snap blew away on a northeast wind, and now we wait and hope the sun gets strong enough to move up the mercury and move down the sap.

As the month comes to a close and April slowly prepares to peek over the horizon, it is time to prepare for the busiest time of all at Lambsquarters. This is the season when my life as a shepherd is all-consuming, overshadowing every other aspect, every trip to town, every visitor, every interruption. Before that happens,

I scurry around to complete chores, to fill the larder, to purchase supplies, to prepare my stable with lambing pens and a communal nursery. I close off an area with a slatted creep gate just wide enough for the anticipated lambs to wiggle through to feed and play away from their dams. I scrub the small water pails and feed buckets, bring the individual hay feeders down from the mow, go through my collection of tags and syringes, rubber gloves and iodine, checking everything off the list. The sheep's calendar, the shepherd's calendar, truly begins the year now.

April

pril mixes memory of lambings arduous and tragic and desire for births gentle and safe. It is far from the cruellest month at Lambsquarters. New lambs bring hope, springing into the world just as the land is reborn. It is the most joyous of months on the farm and the most fretful. The most vibrant and the most lethargic, for there are early mornings, late nights, all-nights in the barn.

First the snowdrops poke through the frozen ground; Galanthus nivalis, whose frosted buds are somnolent under March's seesaw snowfalls and thaws, begin to stand tall and consider opening when April arrives. More robins appear — just the males at first — in flocks of five or six. They fruit the bare apple trees with brightly puffed breasts, preparing their wooing songs for impending females. The bluebird, most favoured of the early arrivals, has not yet appeared, kept back by the late north winds and frozen ground. He will search out a nesting box soon and sing in a mate if he can.

In the barn, everything is reconfigured. The ram, Hunter, moved to a central pen for shearing, is taken back to his lodging in the south alcove, and his temporary pen is forked out, scraped, and dismantled. A nursery of gates and hurdles lies empty, waiting for the first ewes with lambs to arrive. Beside Hunter, we create a creep pen sectioned by a small metal gate. The spaces between its adjustable vertical bars are set at their smallest width, just large enough for the newborn lambs (when they arrive) to slip through into a small pen only for them. They will take refuge there, or make mischief, or wander in accidentally and frantically find themselves away from their dams until they figure it out. This is their pen. They will creep in; they will creep back out.

Along the north wall, I set up the lambing pens, sometimes called claiming pens, jugs, or (my favourite) mothering-up pens. These are hinged gates, four by four feet, which line up in a row against the stone wall. Each will have its own water bucket tied in, a grain pail that fits temporarily over the side, and a small handmade wooden hay feeder with angled slats and a feed-bag backing. These are tricky to attach securely with binder twine, but Thomas has taught me surgical knots to make them stay.

Everything is ready. I bring supplies from the house: rubber veterinary gloves that come up to my shoulder, woollen mittens for traction on slippery lambs' legs during a difficult delivery, iodine for disinfectant, old towels to dry and stimulate a dozy newborn, ear tags for identification, baby scales. And all I can do now is watch and wait.

And cook. I prepare for the constant demand to be in the cold barn by stocking up on easy meals to grab when we have the chance. Each summer, I make my own cherry tomato sauce from the harvest filled with onions and garlic, parsley and basil. I also make my own pesto. I freeze them in small packets for easy pasta sauces to make quick hearty meals, and use them to flavour soup filled with preserved tomatoes, green Slenderette beans, Homesteader peas, and Nantes carrots, shredded because they were missed in the early harvest and grew too big and tough. They are excellent in soup, as are the grated zucchinis I've frozen. Lots of onions and garlic and potatoes from the root cellar also go into the large pot of soup I make. It's always available. And if there's too little time to bake bread, I make soda bread, savoury muffins, or cornbread. We need energy and warmth. And comfort too after sleepless nights. Reward for success and consolation for loss.

With most of the snow melted, it is a time to reconnoitre and inspect winter changes. Fences to repair, shrubs to prune, deadfall to collect. All can wait for warmer days, but along the fencerows, the nesting boxes must be cleared before the bluebirds arrive. The male perches on the power lines, the barn lightning rods, or a tall branch of the backyard maple, but his favourite spot is on top of one of the seven nesting boxes situated around Lambsquarters. He pops in and out, evaluating each one, and frequently shifts among them, but he will eschew any that are already full. In my inspection, I find detritus from a variety of previous occupants. Wrens are notorious for property speculation. They fill every nesting box they can find with small sticks, sometimes right to the ceiling. If they actually decide to take up residence, they build a rather fine small grassy nest on top of the twigs, but frequently they just prevent anyone else from finding a place to settle. Dewallopers.

In my walkabout, I find three boxes filled to the brim, even spilling out the entry, with wren twigs. A fourth has a wren stack on top of a previous bluebird nest — complete with an unhatched egg — then triple-decked with a winter mouse nest. Another is reversed, with a bluebird nest built over a partial wren assemblage. Sadly, this one has three tiny dead fledglings from last year, the blue in their immature feathers still iridescent. With all of them now cleaned out, I can do nothing more than resume my wait.

Waiting is the essence of midwifery. I know the date I put my ram with my ewes, and the average gestation for Border Leicester sheep is 147 days, so I can calculate when the first lambs could arrive. There was a time when we put a marking harness on the ram before breeding. When he mounted the ewe, a coloured crayon left a stain on her back, clearly indicating their recent frolic. But we sell all our wool to handspinners now, and though the crayon washes out, it is unsightly and spoils the presentation of a beautiful rolled fleece. Ultrasound is available for pregnancy testing, and roaming technicians travel from farm to farm with their equipment in a portable case. A screen shows the lambs inside and predicts the state of development. Scans validate the ram's potency; they identify the number of fetuses.

But as I age, and spend more and more time on the farm, I find it unnecessary to establish an exact due date. I'm not keen on catching the ram and tipping his great bulk over to strap him into a harness he's not keen on wearing, and I don't remember changing the crayon colour after the eighteen-day breeding cycle as particularly rewarding. The two-pronged pin that fits through the bracket and the crayon tends to catch halfway along, and while I would try to fish it through, the ram would lose patience. He's got a job to do. He's eager to do it. He'd rather not delay.

With experience, we've learned to predict with reasonable accuracy when a ewe is likely to lamb. Different breeds present differently, but though we started with black-faced crosses, we've had Border Leicesters for over thirty years, so we've come to learn their proclivities. When labour is imminent, it's usually easy to detect. The lambs drop into the pelvis, leaving obvious hollows in the ewes' sides. If we didn't shear prior to lambing, it would be much harder to see, as would the udder development. Thomas has observed that an udder extending well beyond the back legs indicates lambing will probably occur within twenty-four hours. He likens this to a medical sign and has given it an eponymous moniker.

During the first stage of labour, the ewe arches her back with contractions and flexes her tail. To keep the animals clean, and prevent summer fly-strike and maggots, we shorten their tails soon after birth. What remains is a couple of inches long and points straight out with contractions. I call this broomsticking, though it could be McLean's sign if I followed the patriarchal pattern of naming.

When birth is close, the ewe will make a nest, pawing the bedding with one front foot, then the other. She often scrapes with great authority, quite frantically, like the proverbial housecleaning frenzy heralding human labour, and sometimes in several spots, distant from where she finally chooses to lamb. It's important to let her find her own place, particularly once the membranes have ruptured. She will smell the fluids and want to stay near.

Once the first stage is over, the cervix dilated, she goes down on her flank and begins to push with contractions, rising and walking between strains. I've noticed over the years that if a ewe frequently alternates her position from one side to the other, she likely has twins.

If everything goes normally, there will be balloons of amniotic fluid preceding the presenting part. We always hope for a tiny pointed hoof to appear next, followed by another hoof, and the tip of a nose coming just behind or between. With each push, more of the lamb is visible until the whole body plops out in a rush of amniotic fluid. The lamb shakes itself into the world, and the ewe nudges and noses it, chuckles a special welcome, and licks it clean. I often enter the pen at this moment. The ewe is very calm and seems unperturbed by my presence, letting me ensure that the lamb's mouth and nose are free of membranes and allowing me to spray its navel with iodine to help dry it and prevent infection.

If we suspect twins, either from her size, her history, or her side-switching, we watch and wait once again. Some ewes will get right down to deliver a twin or a triplet, but others are so involved with the beloved first-born, they seem to ignore their symptoms until a second lamb is already at the outlet. I've watched a second lamb dangle from a standing ewe more than once. They tend to fall fairly gently to the straw, shake themselves, then bleat to get their mother's attention.

Usually a ewe will shake (her body first, her head and ears last) when she has finished lambing, but this is not a reliable sign. When I feel sure she's done, I move the ewe and her lambs to the mothering-up pen where they will continue to bond, where I can closely watch them, where they are away from distractions or interruptions from the rest of the flock.

The first lambing of the year is always exciting and worrying. Even after so many springs, I'm overcome with emotions going into the season. I have done my preparations, I'm ready, but just like giving birth myself many years ago, the outcome is still unknown, the dangers exist, the responsibility begins. The first ewe this year is a young one who lost her lamb last year. I tend to give them another chance. She's a particularly beautiful ewe with a good disposition and a lovely fleece, so I am not prepared to lose her. My patience pays off as she produces a striking set of twin ewe lambs, born spontaneously, who are lively and well-loved. She has lots of milk, and I have every hope that her progeny will stay in the flock for many years.

The next lambing, by an older ewe, black with a silver fleece, seems to be taking a long time. I'd noted that she'd had a long first stage in the past, so I determine not to worry — not to intervene. Eventually when she does get down and start to push, I observe a tiny hoof. All well. Until I realize it is a *back* hoof. Front feet come out right side up; back feet are upside down. This animal is determined to back into the world, and reverse is not their best gear.

I've seen a small lamb born breech without assistance, but I rarely let that happen. I fear the umbilical cord will break or be constricted in the birth canal, which not only cuts off its oxygen supply but also causes the lamb to try to breathe. With its head still swimming in fluid, it will surely aspirate and die. So seeing these back feet is a clue to get in and help. The ewe, Bess, makes no objection and quietly lets Thomas hold her while I gently draw out the lamb, two long legs quickly followed by the long body and finally the head and forelegs. The backwards lamb takes a breath, bleats, and is received by a clearly relieved ewe. She takes her time with it, licks it clean. It feeds eagerly. But she doesn't shake. And she is still a size. Finally, after almost an hour, she arches her back, broomsticks her tail, gets down, and begins to push. A tiny hoof. Another tiny hoof. But as the dewclaws emerge, it is clear that these too are back feet. This time, I hold her as Thomas delivers another large breech ram lamb, this one black with a white blaze. We are glad to have watched, helped, and have healthy lambs from a treasured ewe.

Just when things seemed to be going well, after several uncomplicated lambings, the first problem appears. A young ewe, her first breeding, takes all morning and into the late afternoon in the first stage of labour. Noting her exhaustion and eager to help, I examine her in the early evening and discover what the books call false ringwomb. The cervix is a tight band after all that labour, barely open. With steady pressure, my hand inside her up to my wrist, well-scrubbed, gloved, and lubricated, I am able to extend the opening considerably. The plan is to wait and examine again later. It is storming, an April blizzard with drifting blinding snow, the wind making me increasingly edgy. After an arduous couple of hours, we manage to deliver a very large live ewe lamb who is floppy, gasping, struggling to breathe. A lamb who would have been an asset to the flock but who's just had too difficult a birth to survive. After all she's been through, the ewe is left lambless, keening in her pen, licking her lifeless progeny.

It makes me want to quit. Even after all the dead lambs we've had to mourn over all the years. There's not much room for sentiment on a farm; we have to be ruthless about culls, and I'm acquainted with veterinary euthanasia. It takes a certain toughness and emotional detachment to be around pain and suffering and inevitable death, but still it breaks my heart. Every time. Thomas's obstetric professor once claimed, "It doesn't matter what you did: if you have a healthy baby and a healthy mother, you did the right thing." I would challenge that aphorism, but for me the corollary is certainly true. If I have a dead lamb, it doesn't matter what I did: I did the wrong thing. I am implicated.

If there were an emotion meter on the farm, the needle would oscillate wildly in April. Some days, I feel that lambing is one-quarter elation and three-quarters misery. After the loss, the next lambing is equally difficult, though we leave her longer before intervening. She continues to strain with no progress and with visible signs of exhaustion, despite evidence of a normal presentation. The feet and head are apparent; they just seem stuck. Another first-timer, another large lamb, another protracted birth. However, this one breathes easily, after our assistance, has a strong sucking reflex, and latches onto the teat before her mother even stands up. The lamb is floppy but alive and eager. Only when we realize she is having difficulty standing do we notice that her right front foot is not working well. It is bent at the first joint, whether from the difficult birth or as a congenital anomaly it hardly matters. She isn't going to be able to support herself.

A lamb must be able to nurse. Either it gets there itself, or I help it, or I give up and put it on a bottle of milk replacer, a specific formula for lambs. And I try desperately not to put a lamb on a bottle. It's critical to get colostrum into a lamb as soon as possible. Antibodies do not cross the placenta as they do in humans, so that first milk is necessary to give them immunity. Because she is so weak, it is difficult to hold her under the ewe at first, so I milk the mother into a syringe and feed the lamb with that. Before the night is over, I milk as much as I can from the ewe and feed the lamb from a bottle with a special lamb nipple. By morning, if I hold her up, she will suck. At least every two hours, that's what we do.

Clearly her foot is not sorting itself out, so I make a splint to set it straight. This is a problem I've seen a couple of times before and one that I treat by using materials at hand. Illustrations show splints made from popsicle sticks, or tongue depressors, but I favour a piece of foam pipe insulation. Stiff enough to hold the leg straight, it is also soft. One side is split to fit around a pipe, so it easily surrounds the foreleg. A bit of self-adhesive wrap, the sort they use on horses, holds it on. Now if I pick her up, she can stand.

But she can't rise, so it still means I'm out there at all hours, picking her up, pointing her in the right direction, and watching that she feeds. The needle on the emotion meter is pointing down. The leg is very weak, and there's no certainty that it will strengthen. Luckily, the ewe is calm and patient. I envy her that. For a shepherd, perseverance is crucial; sleeplessness is unavoidable; frustration is constant.

And spring is recalcitrant this year. Snow just won't stop falling; temperatures refuse to rise. An early morning birth leaves me shivering for hours after I've hastily thrown thin coveralls over pyjamas for the dawn check. Often, if I find a ewe in labour, I return to the house and put on extra layers. But arriving mid-delivery, I must rush to clear the airway of a newborn and soon find myself covered in the copious birth fluids of a healthy set of twins. When I check this older ewe for milk, it will not let down. I keep stripping the teats, which frequently get blocked with a waxy plug, but get nothing. Finally, with one last tug, I am suddenly covered by a powerful spray of colostrum. Freezing temperatures plus lots of liquid plus thin clothing chills to the bone. But the healthy lambs raise the needle on the emotion meter.

The nursery pen is filling up. When the mothers rush the feeders at chore time, the lambs go wild, high jumping on all four feet at once, chasing each other, ducking in and out of the creep pen. They run at speed from one end to the other, do mid-air U-turns, and race back. When I add fresh straw, rather than spread it around, I throw in large wedges and let the lambs do the work. They explore the piles like climbers on uncharted hills. They bounce and gambol and bunt the piles until the fresh straw covers the whole pen.

Every year has its surprises and trials, its triumphs and elations. Farming is about tenacity. I can't just give up after a bad session. But some years, it's difficult to remember a good season. This is one of those years.

Despite a pen full of healthy lambs and dams, the difficulties stay with me. In the middle of the month, just when the fields are clear and the promise of spring is palpable, the snowdrop flowers suddenly retreat under unseasonable snowstorms; early crocuses are iced with layers of freezing rain. Open pastures and gravel tracks disappear after a week-long session of ice and snow that knocks out power lines and socks in laneways. An east wind penetrates the slatted stable doors, seeps in through my coveralls, and batters the animals inside. We put straw bales against the claiming pens, insulating the new lambs, but ice pellets strafe my face as I travel frequently between house and barn. We go to bed with flashlights and headlamps handy, ready to light up the barn when the power goes out. Luckily it doesn't happen until daylight.

Healthy lambs can survive the cold as long as they feed shortly after birth. It's the compromised ones — those whose journey through the birth canal is interrupted or disproportioned, those cases of dystocia that delay the process — who are at greatest risk. Young ewes with large single lambs, malpresentations, and older multiparous ewes with numerous lambs all contribute to the difficulties. And this year, we have them all. Some of them we save; all of them we deliver.

A breech presentation begins backwards with a tail, a rump, or a hind foot coming first. Usually both back feet appear, and carefully controlled traction results in a successful delivery. I've had tail presentations, where the lamb's body must be moved back against the poor ewe, who just tries to push it out, but once the lamb is pushed back, I've been able to convert the presentation by finding the feet and gently pulling them through. One footling breech gives me pause. A lamb with only one hind foot in the birth canal and with the other hip back increases its body's diameter such that it will most likely get stuck. And that umbilical cord cannot be compressed. With my vet gloves on, I carefully follow the lamb's body up the side of the hidden leg and find its knee joint, bent forward, the rest of the leg much farther up, its foot folded against its hip. With one finger, I loop around the hoof, twist it slightly, and unpack the leg until it is coming straight. By pulling gently on both legs, turning slightly as the body follows, I'm able to deliver the lamb quickly enough that its first inspiration is air, not fluid.

A good save is a very large lamb coming headfirst with no feet presenting. Unlike human neonates, whose heads are so large and round, lambs' heads are slim and streamlined. The greatest diameter is over their shoulders. If both front legs are at attention, the pelvis will undoubtedly block any progress. So once again, I am tasked with pushing the presenting part back inside, this time all the way to the uterus, my whole plastic-sleeved arm inside the disconsolate ewe, until I can find first one leg and then much farther back the other, bring them both forward (without having the head fall back), and gently bring it all out into the open. A big ram lamb, happy to be out; a very tired, shaky ewe, quick to claim her progeny; and an exhausted shepherd at two o'clock in the morning, soaked to the skin, shivering.

After a night like this, I rethink my reasons for shepherding. Thomas and I have retired from our off-farm professions. Is it time to think about jettisoning the sheep? I muse on the idea of a dry flock, like Aunt Dorothy's after she sold her hill farm in New Zealand. She kept wethers (neutered rams) for their fleece when the price of wool was high. Surely we could maintain a flock just for their wool, though we would lose money here where winter feed has its costs. I can bring in the price of one lamb on an individual fleece, but giving up market lamb income would be a big loss, where twins double the take. And how much would I miss the lambs, gambolling in the fields when they're first let out? Jumping sky high at dusk; bleating pitifully for their mothers when they think they're lost?

Or we could give up the flock altogether and buy in a summer stock of weaned lambs to fatten on pasture. It would keep our grass down; we wouldn't need to make hay; we could spend more time off the farm in the winter. But what would we be getting? Would I feel the same satisfaction with a commercial mixed flock that I get with my noble Border Leicesters? I love their Roman noses, their long white legs, their lustrous crimped locks. What diseases would we buy in, after all our years of a quarantined closed flock?

And what of the barn? All the work of it; the feeders, the heated water bowls, the henhouse, the cat. Greenwood is integral to the barn. She is our gamekeeper for predator control. The only mice I see are corpses laid out for my approval. And weasels are not beyond her. I once found a headless rabbit on the feed room floor, Greenwood purring her pride nearby. Making her a housecat would be similar to moving me to the city. And it would hardly be worthwhile keeping the water on for two layers and a puss. So would I have to buy eggs? Would the roof fail, the eavestroughs rust away, the siding cave in? These then are the questions facing the aging shepherd. And the answers elude, so it's easier to amend.

I think about changes to make next year better. We could lamb later if April insists on behaving like January. We swore never to lamb in January, but somehow we've managed to do it now the climate has turned inside out. We could feed less grain in the six weeks before lambing, hoping the lambs would be smaller and less likely to get stuck. We could ultrasound the ewes for more exact due dates and multiples and plan accordingly. We can acquire a new ram to cover more ewes in a season, for Hunter seems to have fallen off the job this year. I now remember that he was off-colour in the summer, ran a small fever, perhaps had pneumonia. The vet put him on a course of antibiotics and he improved, but maybe his sperm count fell, or perhaps he's lost the urge. Viagra's not an option.

And I notice that my writing just turned grammatically from the conditional to the present. Not yet giving up. There have been good years, even amazing years. The year we had a 200 percent lambing. The year every ewe delivered within a two-week period. The hundreds of easy lambings and happy ewes. The joy of new life on a warm day. Elation and misery battle it out year by year. Perhaps next time will be better.

I remember a couple who came to farming shortly after we did. They were incredibly enthusiastic, did everything themselves. They purposely bought a cow with a dry quarter, thinking they wouldn't need so much milk. They saved their eggshells, dried them on the wood stove, and ground them into powder to fertilize their garden. The first year was brilliant. Everything grew, everything lived, farming was stellar. Then a bad year followed. The cow died, the lambs sickened, the hens stopped laying, the garden failed. And they sold up and left. Cut their losses, no doubt, and went on to something else. If we all did that, there would be no farmers. So I guess we'll make changes, try to improve.

꿌ᘏ

We are asked to host a tour for people interested in starting sheep farms. In the good weather before lambing, I spend hours preparing. Washing the barn windows, whisking cobwebs from the ceiling, scrubbing water bowls, sweeping the mow. We are to outline our operation, talk about our history, our business plan and our future goals, our marketing and management strategies, and what we'd do differently if we had to do it again.

I agree out of neighbourliness, and perhaps a certain sense of pride, but soon begin to wonder what there is to learn here. Going over the list of questions and anticipating reactions to Lambsquarters gives us the opportunity to examine just what it is we are doing, why, what will happen in the future, and what we might change. We've stuck it out, but at the inevitable tail end of our farming perhaps we are mixing experience with decrepitude.

We consider how farm communications have changed dramatically since we began. In the early years, if one of us needed the other, we had to run from barn to house and yell. When we renovated, we installed an outside light fixture with one spot facing the sheep courtyard, the other aimed toward the house. Our simplistic code was to turn on the light only if there was a need for the other to attend. In the middle of the night, it meant getting up to look out the window for the signal. It occasionally worked.

From there, we moved to an intercom system. Like early baby monitors, one unit stayed in the house and the other in the barn. Mostly it conveyed static, like a message from another planet. But static meant something was happening: better go see. Walkie talkies came next, fancy little appliances with orange toggles, a choice of relay channels and clearer speakers. Over and out. Ten-four. Rather like ship to shore. Then, inevitably, cellphones arrived at the farm. The early models were primitive, but we could actually talk to each other, get our message across. And now we have better ones with great texting and talking power. The only concern is if Thomas texts me when I'm in the barn. It instantly arouses the sheep from their reveries because I've downloaded sheep talk as his text tone. It took me some time to find just exactly the right sounds. Sheep don't all sound the same. The baaing had to mimic my Border Leicesters, and it does that all too well. They perk up their ears, look at me quizzically. Where are these other sheep? It sets up a baa chorus.

If we were younger, just starting, we might put in a camera. Barns are frequently monitored now remotely. The farmer can watch what's happening from miles away on a cellphone, or from the warmth of the fireside on a laptop or tablet. It would have been tremendously handy during the ice storm when I practically needed skates to check the barn safely. Could have saved a lot of unnecessary treacherous trips.

Even more impressive is a device now used on cows, but not, at this time, available for sheep. It's a small computer that attaches around the cow's tail, like a bracelet, to detect when labour is present. An alert is sent to the farmer's cellphone to hotfoot it to the barn for a delivery. We'd have to leave longer tails to make this work on sheep, but no doubt something similar will eventually be available. Called a Moocall, I expect it's not too much of a stretch to imagine a future Ewecall.

We are quite low-tech at Lambsquarters. I keep all my records in a binder, adding contemporaneous notes by hand. Our lambing records are in two places: a pocket diary in the barn for immediate lambing information — time of birth, weight of lambs, type of delivery — and on yellow cardstock sheets in my binder. Each ewe has her own sheet with her biography and pedigree on the front, her yearly lambing record on the back. The first computer sheep programmes available were awkward, and the current ones can be expensive. For our small flock, this antiquated system suffices. But it certainly dates us.

On the whole, we tend to eschew mechanization. We haul small square bales by hand, individually water ewes in their claiming pens, and use a fork and a wheelbarrow to clean them out. And we are not keen on interference at lambing. I prefer to approach a birthing problem as a midwife, not an obstetrician.

The last ewe to lamb this year is Ailsa, a ten-year-old crossbred ewe at the end of her career who looks as if she might challenge my midwifery skills. I'm not sure why I kept her to begin with: she is not ever going to provide replacement ewes, and her fleece is more the North Country Cheviot (a shorter bulkier down wool) of her sire than the silky lustrous Border Leicester of her dam. But she's consistently produced great market lambs, and she's something of a character. I spun her wool one year and made a cabled cardigan, dyed cerulean like a Caribbean cove. We've had an entre nous arrangement this year. Because she's lost a lot of condition over the winter, I feed her extra. She goes to the same exact feeder spot each evening for her supersized helping of oats and molasses. Despite the attention, she looks skinnier and scrawnier each day, her backbone clearly evident under her shorn wool coat. I've kept her too long, but all I can do now is continue to feed her and hope for the best.

As the others lamb and move through the claiming pens and into the nursery, Ailsa is still with the unbred — the yearlings and the few ewes who had not conceived. With no need to feed a grain ration to the others, I move her into a double claiming pen to await her confinement. She has lots of space, a neighbour in the next pen, and no animals to compete with for food. I increase her ration and give her oats and molasses twice a day, plus a malt tonic to keep her strength up for the lambing ahead.

The day arrives that she goes off her food. A slight arching suggests early labour, but after many hours with no progress, I begin to fret that she is either experiencing pregnancy toxaemia or hypocalcaemia. If toxic, the ewe has so little reserve that she begins to break down body tissues to keep up with the growth of the lambs, and if hypocalcaemic, it's calcium that is leached from her system. Either can be fatal, and both must be treated quickly. I try to get a urine sample to check for ketones, which would be present if she is breaking down body tissues, but pulling on her nose, which sometimes works, fails to give me a drop. It is time to call the vet.

After a telephone conversation, we agree to give her calcium, which will do no harm and might help, and to watch and wait. Eventually I do get a urine sample and find no ketones. Definitely good news. The books suggest a very poor survival rate unless the ewe lambs quickly. But still no progress. She arches her back, broomsticks her tail, but infrequently and with little conviction. And still she does not eat. After further consultation, the vet determines to come to the farm to see for herself and discuss our options. Ailsa is not dilating and by then is showing fewer contractions. She still seems relatively bright, perhaps perked up by the malt tonic and calcium, but things look pretty grim. She is so thin, and I fear that if she gets through the lambing, she might not survive. Quite apart from the fear of losing her, this is the last lambing, and so far I have no babies on bottles. I do not want an orphan.

The vet says that if this were her sheep, she'd do a caesarean section. Our only other option is to give Ailsa steroids to induce labour and hope for the best. But the prognosis is not good: if she doesn't lamb within twenty-four to thirty-six hours, she'll still likely need a section, and by then, we are told, the lamb could be dead. I just don't want to put this old sheep through the pain of surgery. And as farmers, we have to be practical rather than sentimental. She is not going to produce a replacement ewe, and she is not going to continue to be a breeder. The economics are against it. Apart from that, I hate to interfere with something so invasive. We elect to induce and wait. And it is a difficult wait.

The endpoint of the vet's time limit will occur in the middle of the night — no time to call her out — so we have to make our decision by four o'clock the following afternoon. Ailsa is still having contractions through the following morning and looking somewhat perkier, but still she is not eating and not pushing. By mid-afternoon, she has made progress: the first balloon of membranes appears. We continue to monitor but do not interfere. Her labour is slow and weak, just a few half-hearted pushes with no obvious progress, until a few hours later she manages to push out another balloon and seems to be pushing harder. We agree to examine to see what we have. A dead lamb? A malpresentation? I feel a nose and behind it one foot. We determine to leave her a little longer — the cervix is still detectable and it needs to thin completely.

After another hour, she is actively pushing. And all we can see is a nose. I am able to find a foot, not too far back, and deliver it forward. Because she is having so much trouble, we don't want to chance delivering the lamb with a foot behind so I push the head back in and feel for the second foot. All I can get is a knee. Ailsa is pushing hard against me, and I can't get my hand in far enough through the pelvis to unpack the leg. I can't reach the hoof. There seems nothing for it but to deliver this little Superman, trying to fly with one arm out, one behind. Frequently a lamb will pull its foot back, indicating liveliness, but there is no movement here. It is a struggle, and I quickly give up and let Thomas take over. My hands are much smaller so I tend to examine and manipulate, but he has the strength, so he does the heavy pulling. I grab the old woollen mitts we use for traction on slippery deliveries and hold Ailsa and soothe her while Thomas pulls and pulls.

Eventually that glorious click sounds as the second shoulder clears the pelvis, and a lovely white ram lamb slithers out. Alive. He shakes his ears, he breathes, he bleats. Ailsa is exhausted, unreactive, on pause. Gone tharn like a rabbit from *Watership Down*. I rub the lamb's back with fresh straw, spray its navel with iodine, check its mouth for sucking reflex. Because she is still down, I am able to milk Ailsa, then lift the lamb onto her teat. He sucks. With vigour!

Shortly afterwards, Ailsa comes to, begins to chuckle, and the bond begins. She gets up, licks him off, and encourages him to get on his feet by gently pawing the straw beside him, gently pawing his back. Splayed, with back legs like a frog, he makes many efforts before finally standing on all four feet, wobbling his way under his mother and searching for sustenance. We've avoided surgery, haven't needed the obstetrician, and have managed with our combined midwifery skills and a good dose of luck. Ailsa is doing very well, continues to enjoy extra rations, and seems particularly fond of her lamb.

I think I'll call him Craig.

May

May drops like nightfall in the tropics this year. But instead of sudden blackness, everything is brilliantly light. From snow flurries to sunshine, spring weather rushes in with a flick of the calendar page. The cruelness of April morphs magisterially into the darling buds of May. And everything changes.

Lambing is over; the tour guests have gone; the snow disappears overnight. After a month filled with anticipation, silently standing still and watching labouring ewes in a frigid barn, waiting for lambs to be born, I'm immediately immersed in frenzied occupation.

The land is waking up. Flocks of birds, gone since the autumn, return in ribbons and orchestrate the dawn. Evensong belongs to the frogs: spring peepers serenade the swamp. Canada geese strut in the swales, swim in the ponds, nest in the bracken of cattail mounds. Cluster flies sunbathe on south-facing walls, fill window panes in the barn, buzz their way outdoors from their winter crevices. And the earth thaws and opens, releases worms and ants and all manner of creeping insects. Honeybees blanket the scilla, their flowers a blue coverlet on the lawn, and tiny violets kindly perfume the grass over the septic bed.

Brown quickly chameleons to green. On the lawn, in the fields, on the lilacs. But all the detritus hidden by winter snows is laid bare. The soggy leaves in the perennial beds, the rotting debris in the vegetable garden, the ice-felled branches from the maples and oaks, orange fronds from the cedars. Piles of sunflower casings litter the ground beneath the bird feeders, and the manure pile in the barnyard melts its rich liquid tea. So much must be cleaned up, cleared away. I'm disheartened after such an inclement lambing, but energized by the sun, the green, the new growth.

We determine to lamb later next year. If unpredictable weather is the only predictable climate, perhaps moving further into spring will help us as we age and weaken. I'm still strong enough to sling hay bales and to hold a reluctant ewe, but just. And I find it much more difficult to survey the barn in the middle of the night, particularly when it's storming and cold. Not having to use snowshoes will make my trips easier. I can time the chores within daylight hours morning and night and eliminate at least one check in the dark.

Lambing later will push all the spring frenzy together. I'll be raking and forking manure, weeding and planting with constant interruptions from the barn. But I won't need to pile into winter jacket, hat, and gloves. I can dispense with the long johns and the sore hands which blanch white in the cold. I will be frantically busy, but I hope to be warmer, happier, more patient. I fear some of our lambs were hauled out precipitously, like human inductions on Fridays, just so I could get back to my fireside.

Warm weather has its own concerns for the shepherd. All the burgeoning insect life provides food for birds and pollinators for plants, but it can be troublesome for sheep. As soon as the temperature rises, nose bots appear. The Oestrus ovis is a pesky little fly that drops off larvae on the sheep's nose once the weather warms up. If left unchecked, the larvae will migrate up the nostrils into the sheep's sinuses, causing discharge and distress. Just when it's nice enough for the animals to head happily into the barnyard sun, these critters appear and chase them back into the barn. The sheep press their snouts into the ground, stamp their feet, shake their heads. Anything to keep the flies from attacking. I expect these flies will be particularly troublesome to a labouring ewe.

The thaw reveals treasures once frozen beneath the snow. There's a scapula bone on the track of my daily walk. From a fox perhaps. It is a strong bone, bleached white, and I walk by it day after day, wondering about its provenance. My own scapulae, protruding now as I wither and age, are unlikely to be so solid. There's a history of porous bones in my family. A series of broken hips in my female line. Both grandmothers, and my mother broke both. Which is one of the reasons I walk and walk. I could be the poster person for osteoporosis as I have all the risk factors except tobacco use. So I don't smoke, and I get lots of weight-bearing exercise for density and strength. I think about tiny holes that may be forming in my bones. But they are not yet lying open on the track. I still surround them.

The first wild plants form a menagerie. Coltsfoot, dogtooth violet or trout lily, horsetail, and pussytoes. They appear in sequence, coltsfoot first, blooming at roadsides, mimicking dandelions, but happily as it has been so long since we've seen any colour. It's named for its hoof-shaped leaf, is an unwelcome weed in farm fields. It thrives in gravel and tends to stay put there at the edges of roads, out of trouble. Dogtooth violet, which is not a violet at all, also has cheery yellow flowers and blooms in the forest. Although its petals are shaped rather like dogs' teeth, it's actually the root that names it. A single tap root, pure white and tapering at a curve, looks uncannily like a dog's canine. But really it is a lily and aptly named *trout* for its brown leaf spots. Whether brown trout or speckled trout hardly matters; the leaves are tapered at both ends, curved and spotted and convincingly fishy.

But the horsetail is the most intriguing of the early sprouters. It is known as a living fossil, the only survivor of the Paleozoic era hundreds of millions of years ago. It looks otherworldly, popping out of the ground with a translucent beige stem with a reticulate horsetail-shaped top. It grows in the wetlands here, straight soft spears about the size of a small asparagus. Then, just when I'm not looking, it turns green and unfolds feathery whorls of leaves and transforms from a horsetail to a soft bottle brush, only to morph once again into a hank of lustrous strands.

Pussytoes are just as they sound. Small tufts of velvety white pads, pushing up from a pale stem, grow in patches on barren ground, as if a clowder of cats lies supine on the meadow, claws drawn in.

Spring plants are ephemeral. Only daily observance catches them in a woodland spectrum from goldthread to greenbrier, blue cohosh to wild indigo, violet violet to fire pink, red trillium to bloodroot. I extend my walk to the next farm, in limbo now since my Dutch neighbours have both died, Gerrit first, felled by fatal illness while working in his bush, and Maik some years later overnight in her own bed. The farm reluctantly presents itself for sale, the next generation conflicted, the son greatly affected by his proximity on the adjacent farm, the daughters more distant. My neighbours to the south are anxious to continue to rent the fields and plant another crop.

This is a difficult change for us. Maik and Gerrit taught Thomas and me so much about farming. We miss them viscerally. Not having older mentors is another of the indignities of aging, not outwardly visible like the sun damage on my skin, the grey of my hair, but deeper, harder, more intense. Their fields behind my barn were planted in permanent pasture, always available to me, a stile built to cross the line fence between us. Now they are freshly planted in corn, and it's only safe to walk there before the kernels sprout. I take myself past the watercress pond filled by an underground spring to the massive beech tree we once dubbed magic. It has a bizarre horizontal branch growing from the main trunk into a parallel tree. A hen and egg conundrum as to what came first. We picnicked there when our children were small. We climbed the elephantine branches. I gave it a chapter in a previous book.

But now one trunk is rotten; those smooth branches decompose on the forest floor. Only the side tree still exists, bravely rising from the detritus. A sad sight, not climbable, no place for a picnic. No neighbours, no magic beech, no bucolic pastures with grazing Holsteins. Change. Inevitable with age, unavoidable.

I carry on, searching for morels, absorbing the sight of so many trilliums, so many spring wildflowers, the sound of so much birdsong.

With the sheep on pasture, my chores suddenly reduce. The animals are so delighted to be eating fresh grass, they seem to have forgotten completely about oats and hay. No longer do they begin a baa chorus as soon as I go out the door, but barely look up from grazing as I count them each morning and night. All winter, the sound of the back door opening set them calling. They baaed incessantly, annoyingly, until fodder was in their feeders. But now I just hear the sound of grazing, the odd bleat of a lamb, a response from a dam.

Sheep graze by cutting grass with their lower front teeth against a hard toothless upper palate. It makes a ripping sound as they travel through the sward. We may not be able to hear the grass grow, but sheep make the grass audible. They give it voice.

※ ※

Just when the chores let up and I've let my guard down, the trouble commences. From the loft window, I look out on the flock as I leave my bed. Something is awry. A black sheep with grey fleece looks peculiar. She's flicking her ears, a normal occurrence as insects are bothersome. But the flicking seems to come from both ends of the sheep. She has a coal-black lamb, so perhaps it's moving, but I'm confused. It just doesn't look right. From the windows downstairs, I can finally interpret the scene. She's stuck on her back, and those aren't ears flapping, nor a lamb dancing about. Those are legs. Four black feet waving around, hopelessly trying to right herself. She's turned turtle. She's cast.

A cast ewe is generally, but not always, in full fleece. The weight of the wool, the slope of the land, the altered centre of gravity of a gravid ewe will infrequently result in an upturned sheep. If left too long, she will suffocate from the buildup of gases in her rumen. Years ago, travelling in Scotland, on our way to meet Thomas's cousins for the first time, I spotted such a ewe in a remote field. He stopped the van and I jumped out, hopped the fence, and turned her over. She trotted off and I was only slightly muddy from the operation. Presentable enough for the relatives. The writer Mary Wesley has a character in one of her novels pull the emergency alarm on a train to do the same. Some of us are just natural sheep Samaritans.

When I realize what is happening, I summon the dog, who is old and creaky but still keen to help, and run out in my pyjamas to find Stella, my biggest, fattest, and now most bloated ewe completely stuck. It takes all my strength to heave her over, but it is too much for me to keep her stable. She immediately jumps up and tries to take off at speed only to be felled by one side of her body that cannot cooperate. Down she goes and over she turns, all lopsided from the bloat in her stomachs, exacerbated by her age and the lack of muscle tone in having carried triplets to term. I heave her back, and again she tries to run. Flora, my collie, gently persuades her from stumbling far, cleverly lying down in front of her whenever she tries to flee. We keep this up for two or three more horrifying displays of incapacity until eventually she trundles off, limping on unsteady legs to the bottom of the paddock, her lambs following at heel. Flora, also looking a bit knackered from her efforts, now stays by my side, job well done. Stella is wet and filthy and clearly distressed, but she is upright. She lets the lambs suck.

All day I check on her every hour, terrified that she's done real damage. The lambs are still too young to be on their own, and I don't want to lose her. Each time I notice small improvements. She is standing still. She is chewing her cud. She is grazing. Always her lambs are with her. I don't see her lie down until the next day, nor can I blame her. It seems we'll get away with it this time. Another close call — another save.

I don't use Flora very often to muster the sheep. They are so well inclined to move from pasture to pasture, so ready to eat fresh grass that they rarely need a push. But if one gets out, or the whole flock heads off in the wrong direction, Flora's instincts are to round them up and bring them back to me. She's a beautiful dog, blue merle with blue eyes. Huge fur. A calm companion, prepared to work if asked.

Birds flock back to Lambsquarters in May. Later this year than usual, but in quick succession. The barn swallows signal the time to spread manure. They are gregarious birds, living in colonies. After a couple of days of one scout resting on the hydro wire, the rest of the crew arrives en masse. They swoop in wild formation in and out of the stable. It is critical to leave the stable doors open, the garage doors shut. They are inside nesters, preferring beams and rafters. Picking up mud from spring puddles in their beaks, they mix it with grass and make pellet bricks and mortar to build semicircular wattle nests on the sides of a barn beam.

Careful engineers, they begin by crafting a small shelf to sit on, then work upwards. The barn and barnyard fill with swooping birds, chattering incessantly as they dip in and out, finding their mud and grass, making connections, mating. I surmise that generations of the same families have nested here for over a hundred years. There are thirteen nests in the barn. They use them over and over again, through the season and year after year. New feather linings and fresh mud rims renovate the nests each spring. When sitting, the swallow is often completely hidden within the nest, but once the hatchlings arrive, the parents perch on a nearby ledge while the young birds arrange themselves in a row, their triangular beaks hanging over the edge like Muppets.

Barn swallows eat insects, up to sixty an hour and over eight hundred a day. Plenty of food to feed their large broods here at Lambsquarters, and lots of action as they zoom up and swoop down to catch their prey. They keep the mosquitoes down for us. Unfortunately, with the decrease in bank barns, swallows find fewer nesting sites. New barns tend to have well-fitting doors, denying access to the birds. The swallows have declined significantly with the dearth of nesting sites, and I expect the neighbouring barn fire will contribute to the problem. They are swooping outside my window as I write, the forked tails of the males evoking the legend that an ancient deity struck them for stealing fire from the gods, destroying the centre tail feathers.

Once the hatchlings fledge, they line up in rows. Greenwood sits mesmerized. She'd dearly love to catch a tender bit of bird flesh, but I've foiled her for a number of years now with her cat bib. I read about the bib in a Jonathan Franzen novel and immediately ordered one. It's a neoprene triangular-shaped contraption that velcros onto a cat collar. Greenwood happily wears it from the beginning of spring to the end of the autumn migration, and I haven't seen her catch a bird since. She can still hunt mice, but the bib defeats her birding. Apparently it works because cats wait for a bird to fly up before they jump to catch it on the ascent. The bib both puts off the cat's attack and startles the bird. It flies off unscathed, and the cat goes back to mousing. I've never seen another cat wearing the bib, and I fear for all the birds needlessly killed.

Despite my disarmed cat, I wait in vain for the song of the meadowlark — her "I am com-ing" call never sounds. It is not only cats who deter the birds: changing climate, lack of habitat, and pesticides all contribute. I may not see a bobolink or hear its chatter this year either. Both species are on the threatened list now, their nesting grounds invaded and depleted by land development, ever earlier hay cuts, heavy cropping, overgrazing, and reforestation. There's a significant lack of meadowlands to provide the high grass prairie they need to raise a brood. They were plentiful here when we first farmed. Now they are rare.

As the month progresses, my walk, the same path I take each day, changes dramatically. Frog song gives way to the birdsong of the many species still plentiful or, in the case of the ruffed grouse, to drumming. It sounds as if a small engine is starting up. Something like an outboard motor used for fishing. Deep in the woods is an unlikely place for such a sound, but it's exactly where the male ruffed grouse beats his wings ever faster to make the noise. I've never seen him do it, but in May I hear him, particularly if I'm out early in the morning. My presence often flushes these mainly ground birds into a startled flight, frightening me just as I've frightened them.

A day before the first blossoms open, I hear an oriole. Such sweet music, high in the maples, he sings in the spring. When the snow melts, an old oriole nest emerges on my path. I first notice it because of a bright blue thread running through. Where once the orioles wove with horsehair, now they mix plastic threads from feed bags and bale twine into their exquisite hanging nests.

One morning early, just as I am getting used to the May sounds, something startles and confuses me. A rustling, whirring sound high up, like a massive flock of birds flapping quickly. I am deep in the wetland woods, surrounded by aspens and oaks, near the pond where the frogs sing and the geese nest. Many of the trees are dead near the water, so I'm used to hearing woodpeckers; downy, hairy, and even pileated woodpeckers work hard hammering into those dead branches for insects and grubs. But this is different. It comes in a whoosh — a rush — like a waterfall. It takes some time to decipher. When I look up, it suddenly becomes clear. For the first time since fall, there are leaves on the trees. A sudden wind sets them astir. Aspen, *tremble* in French, flapping individually, collectively playing the wind, an aeolian harp in the sky.

🌾 🌾

When the days lengthen and the soil thaws, it's time to plant the vegetable garden. The enthusiasm of youth has dwindled to the point where I start only a few things inside now, and not until early May, just to give them a head start. Some of this is a lack of energy, but experience also brings wisdom. Without a greenhouse or artificial light setup, I can't produce very strong plants in the house, and I've winnowed down to what works for me and what I like to grow.

Brassicas attract cabbage butterflies. They are white or yellow and quite pretty, but their larvae grow into voracious green caterpillars who make lace of the plants. It takes far too much patience or noxious chemicals to control them, and I now have neither. They are banished. Tomatoes grow better now that the climate is warmer and frosts are later, but I don't like their smell and never seem to control full-sized ones in their cages, so they too have been turfed from the garden. Instead, I start little Sweety cherry tomatoes in the house and plant them out on stakes against a fence in a separate patch. I'm able to prune them into one straight central stem, keep them orderly and productive. I've settled now into a routine of old favourites.

Years ago, I followed a Mennonite woman around the farm co-op, where they sell seeds in wooden bins, with scoops to fill paper bags. I had no idea what corn to buy, what peas, what onions. So I watched her and bought what she bought. I've never seen a Mennonite garden that wasn't beautiful, huge, and productive, so I knew she'd know. Instead of the sweet-looking Early Frosty or Little Marvels from the seed catalogue, I followed her lead and scooped up a bag of Homesteader peas. I've been growing them ever since, and they are one of the first seeds to go into the garden as soon as I can work the soil. Dutch onion sets go in right away with arugula and Grand Rapids, Buttercrunch, and Ruby Red lettuces, and Bloomsdale Long Standing spinach. These can all go in before the last frost, but I wait until the twenty-fourth of May to set out the tender plants and seeds, the Peaches and Cream corn, Slenderette bush beans, delicata and acorn squash, Small Sugar pumpkins.

Before the garden can be worked, I start by drawing up a plan on paper. My garden is basically square and is divided into quarters diagonally to make four triangles. Thomas made a large wooden obelisk trellis in the centre for morning glories, and leading to it are four flagstone paths planted with creeping thyme. My friend Sarah kindly placed the paths for me when my arm was broken, sourcing the stone from a local quarry. Each year I rotate the plants, checking back on last year's plan to remind me what was where. This helps preserve the soil nutrients: corn depletes nitrogen, whereas peas fix it into the ground. I shift the carrots each year to foil the rust fly, and I plant arugula under a floating row cover in a small patch less than a metre long to ward off the flea beetles who would otherwise redesign it into delicate green lace. I bend hoops of number 9 wire to make a canopy for fabric that lets in light and moisture but keeps bugs out. A length of old chain around the perimeter holds it down.

Gardening is all about the future. We have an oak tree in the front lawn that is forty feet high. Originally transplanted as an infant sapling from my father's house, it easily fit in the trunk of his car. The trees we plant now are an investment in someone else's future. With vegetables, the wait is shorter, but there are no guarantees. Either they — or we — might not make it to harvest! Weeds, weather, disease, pests. Anything can happen. And still I plan on paper, mapping out what to grow, where to situate, and when to plant. I fight the slugs and chipmunks by planting beans and corn inside large plastic drinking cups with the bottoms cut out. I use old netted sheep fencing to support my peas and still hesitate to touch it even though it hasn't been connected to an electric fencer for years. Its shocking days are over.

The dags from shearing, those soiled bits from the back end of the sheep, and the belly wool go between the rows of raspberries planted in the pig garden on the first decent day in spring. It is a small square plot in front of the driveshed where one summer we kept two weaner pigs until they were big enough for the freezer. We got the idea in New Zealand, where everyone we knew seemed to have a garden pig fed on table scraps. With small children at the time, we had an abundance of peanut butter crusts and leftovers to fatten them, so Thomas built an enclosure. It was an experience we did not repeat. I don't think any of us actually warmed to these animals, despite how clever they are. And it turned out we aren't great fans of pork. So now the pigpen is the raspberry garden and produces a wonderful crop each year with little effort. Most raspberry varieties bear on the previous year's canes, but I've planted the Red River strain that, while later, grows on the same year's stem. This means I can keep the rows well controlled and cut everything down at the end of the season rather than having to prune out prickly bushes while leaving the new growth behind. Easier to handle and less work.

The main vegetable garden is just south of the barn. Manure mixed with snow and ice in the barnyard melts into a rich nutrient tea right into the garden, and I expect I have earliest and perhaps biggest rhubarb plants in the county.

Recently I've been curtailed on two of the garden edges as Thomas replaces the old page-wire fence with drystone walls. His stonemasonry began some years ago with barn foundation repairs, moved rapidly into a mortared fieldstone wall at the foot of the lane, and has culminated in an obsession with drystone dyking. He took a weekend course and soon rocks began to accumulate.

Thomas hand-dug a foundation for a roadside wall 135 feet long and began to place stones. It was a brave venture to place a novice drystone structure in plain view. I've been told that back in the days when farmers routinely ploughed their fields — before air-seeding and no-till cropping — the rookies learned their craft on the back forty. Only the experienced put their perfect work on show.

It took him a couple of summers to complete, and quite a bit of consternation, but Thomas crafted a beautiful landmark. The batter isn't quite what it might be; the base not especially wider than the cap; it needs frequent repairs in spots. But it is a work of art. A touchstone.

Several projects since, including a lengthy stone snake farther along the road and a sinuous fieldstone wall that meanders through the trees between fields named Muir and Swaledale, he is now working on a functioning fence around my vegetable garden. By now, he's mined most of the exposed rock on the farm, every year adding the newly frost-heaved stones. As we live on rolling glacial moraine, it's remarkable to have used up so many stones. Some claim it's the township's best crop. Certainly the earliest.

Rarely do we drive on a country road without a stop for some precious piece of granite just the right size or shape. If he's gone to town for supplies and seems to take forever, I expect him to return with the back of the truck weighed down with rocks he just couldn't resist collecting along the way. Stones always find their way into his luggage when we travel and are brought as precious offerings by visitors from away.

Thomas's initial plan was to replace a failing wire fence on the west side of my garden with drystone. He worked on it all last summer, carefully measuring the batter and height to keep animals in the field and out of the vegetables. It is next to a small paddock where we keep our ram, so the wall needs to be strong enough to resist his bunts and scratching. There can't be any loose stones or weak spots for the ram to find. When I watch Thomas work, I see he does as much planning as placing. It is a mixture of geometry, philosophy, and brute strength. Like a cryptic crossword puzzle, the wall grows through intense contemplation and finesse.

This summer, Thomas is less of a rockhound. After the neighbour's barn burned down in March, nothing was left but the foundation. A beautiful fieldstone foundation surrounding ash and rubble. As they began the cleanup, the neighbours kindly asked if Thomas would like some stones for his dyking. And so they arrived. Three large truckloads. These stones were hand-picked, hand-split, and hand-placed over a hundred years ago. They kept the weather out, the animals in. Generations of stock were born, milked, nurtured within their shelter. And now, thanks to the kindness of neighbours, they will have a new role in my garden, for Thomas is rebuilding the corner and extending the wall along the south fenceline. I can only hope it will continue to advance along the other sides in future. He surely has enough stone.

I can watch the wall grow from my writing hut perched above the barnyard on the extended bank of the original barn. I see the inside growing in courses and marvel at Thomas's skill in placing the stones to shed water and cleave together with nothing more than careful placement, shape, and gravity. I can watch him hold a stone and let it rest pleasantly in his hand as he pauses and absorbs its heat. The stones range in colour from greys through blue and green to pink and almost white. Where the stones are newly split, mica shines in a shower of mirrored dots catching the sun. There are no machines involved in this work, but it is not silent. When he splits a rock or shapes a stone, there's a melodic rhythmic pinging as he taps the stone wedge with the splitting hammer. His patient, steady song gently persuades the stone to shift shape. The tone varies with the type and size of rock but is always pleasant. A comforting ostinato.

Quite apart from the joy of having a beautiful wall around my veggies, I am looking forward to climatic benefits. The rocks hold warmth and give me a boost in heat units. Because of our elevation on the Dundalk Plain, we are in the same climate zone as parts of northern Ontario. We show on a climate map as an isolated dot surrounded by better growing conditions. The stones give the garden a warmer microclimate.

Perched on a hill with open access to the west, the garden is directly in the path of prevailing winds that can topple taller plants like peas on the vine and corn. The stone wall now provides a solid windbreak. Already this year, I see an improvement, as my pea fences, which often need guy wires to keep them upright, are standing unsupported within the shelter of the wall.

Giving new purpose to these foundation stones ensures the survival of their beauty. Instead of being bulldozed into oblivion, they are being reconfigured into another useful handcrafted structure around the corner from their first use since the glacier deposited them. They rise again from the ashes into a phoenix wall.

June

The early blossoms of May profuse in June. From the golden plum, the first to unbud, there's a steady progression through the various fruit trees to the lilacs, berries, and ornamentals. Apples, cherries, crabapples, pears, dogwood, elderberry, hawthorn, chokecherry, raspberries, blackberries, honeysuckle, and mock orange all bloom on the farm. The air is full of fragrance. During a windstorm petals fall like snow.

The lambs grow quickly on pasture and venture farther from their mothers to find choice grass. The ewes let them wander, calling them back at lengthening intervals for ever shorter nursing moments, as if they just want reassurance the lambs haven't strayed too far. As they get bigger, twins bunt the udder so aggressively to get the milk to let down, they can lift a ewe's back legs off the ground. They wag their tails in time as they suck, their front legs kneeling to reach the teats.

Too often the lambs graze greedily, completely unaware of the rest of the flock, then look up and cannot find their dams. Their baaing is both desperate and forlorn, as if they've been abandoned for life. Eventually they find their mothers, though as the month progresses it seems the ewes are less likely to return their calls, enjoying their own increasing freedom.

Frequently there's an escape artist. This year it's Craig, the youngest and smallest lamb. He's the one who notices when the fencer is turned off or shorted out by long wet grass along the fence-row. He's nimble enough to jump between strands and small enough to find a space between rails. I find him on the front lawn testing out greener grass and eyeing my flower beds. I chase him back through the gate, then put some spare lattice panels along the wider spots in the rail fence. He goes along the entire paddock testing each section until he finds a tiny area on one edge of the lattice. As I watch, he gets his head and one foot through and I figure he's going to get stuck, but undeterred, he wiggles and pushes and manages to get both shoulders through, both front legs, and the rest follows easily. Perhaps his difficult birth taught him perseverance.

In June, the hens move to their summer residence. Their summer cottage. It is a small pine chicken house surrounded by a good-sized chain-link dog kennel where they can eat grass and bugs and make depressions in the earth for dust baths. There's a spacious nest, a roost, a fenced run within, and lots of extra open space in the kennel. Generally I open the door and let them run free during the day once they've adjusted to the laying box. I don't want to search for eggs under bushes and behind buildings. They do an excellent job of hunting insects, and they are amusing to watch strutting around. The yolks gain colour and flavour as they vary their diet outside.

I see an alarming mass of feathers strewn about the kennel as I approach one morning to feed them and let them out. One of the two hens, Lucy, is alone on the grass. Maureen isn't with her. They are named after famous redheads for the colour of their feathers: one orange, the other auburn. I fear the worst: that a predator has invaded. I've known weasels to kill chickens, and once a raccoon ripped the chicken wire right off the pen when the hens were inside the barn. But weasels are quick and sly and don't tend to leave a lot of feathers about, and chain link should exclude a raccoon.

Maureen is not dead but cowers safely in the laying box, apparently unhurt. And that's where she stays for the next few days, unsettled. Chicken PTSD. The number of feathers on the ground seems excessive and includes wing quills as well as lots of down. All I can imagine is that something frightened them so much that they flapped and flayed and loosened their feathers in fear. I decide not to let them roam.

Later that afternoon, I catch a glimpse of a reddish creature loping through the field behind the barn. I quietly approach and arrive at the pen at the same time it does. A slinking fox is back to eye its prey. It takes one look at me and flies across the field and over the fence in a single bound. But then I remember hearing a bark earlier that morning. It's raspier than a dog, short and sharp. It's a sound you can hear in an outdoor night-time scene in any British film or television mystery. Ubiquitous on the soundtrack, but not common here at Lambsquarters. We see foxes occasionally and have had a few dens over the years, but I don't remember ever hearing them bark. Since then, I am wakened each night by barking foxes, and I lock the hens into their house, doubly caged.

Maureen recovers. She moves out of the nesting box and after a few days begins again to lay. I haven't seen the fox near the kennel again, but each morning two kits cavort in the field across the road where I start my walk, or crouch on the gravel. They bat each other about, play a kind of fox tag, tussle like puppies or kittens. I see them in the evening if I sneak over to look, and as long as they don't come back to my hens, I'm delighted to have them. They are wonderful mousers, and my barn cat is getting old. She can use neighbourhood assistance.

❦❧

We acquired our first dog by accident. Quite literally. A hound-shepherd mix, she had been hit by a car. A puppy with a broken hip. With owners unprepared to pay a vet, she needed a home in a hurry and we were available and willing. We put no thought into it, just took the dog. Thomas named her Jessie. After weeks with her hind leg bound to her body, she regained full use of the hip; the only sign was at full gallop when the leg went around without touching the ground.

Jessie moved with us to the farm. Our first livestock. Immediately she took to the fields, mastered the fences. Nothing stopped her. She approached a snake fence at top speed, turned sideways in the air, and flew through between the rails.

After fourteen years, one day Jessie was just gone. Whether she got into livestock and was quietly dealt with, or she was picked up, or just took herself off, we'll never know.

Our first year here, she had puppies with the neighbour's Samoyed. Silver was said to be the best groundhogger in the township. We kept Zoë from the litter, and she lived up to the legacy, keeping the groundies out of the garden, but unfortunately she liked to bring them near the house when decomposed. A fine scent to roll around in.

Dogs get old so fast. After Zoë died, we felt we should get a proper sheepdog. Fiona was an Australian shepherd, a breed known for its herding instinct. She had a great talent for rounding up sheep, but I am not much of a trainer. Trying to teach her to "come bye" for left, or go "away to me" to the right, taxed my own direction abilities. By the time I figured out the command, she was off running and so were they. She did obey "that'll do," and I spent a lot of time with that one, just getting her to stop. I've since learned that "come bye" cues the dog to go around the flock clockwise, "away to me" counter-clockwise. I might have done better had I understood that then.

Fiona was a very independent dog. She lived mostly outside, preferring to be covered in snow under the cedar trees to being mollycoddled in the house. These dogs love to work; they need to be busy. Occasionally she would go on a tear and run around the perimeter of the house over and over for the fun of it. She was a faithful companion and lived to be sixteen when a stroke took her off. Thomas was away when she died. My daughter helped me bury her near a bush she loved to lie under on hot summer days. Hard work.

It took a year before I was ready to get another. I might not have been ready then, but Thomas and our son found Adelaide, another Aussie, and picked her for her beauty. A black tricolour, she had a lovely silky coat and a long feathered tail. Addie was boisterous and nervous, an anxious dog. She too loved to herd, and I did use her to bring in the flock. Once in behind them, she did an excellent job and seemed to know exactly where I wanted her to take them.

After Adelaide died, I wasn't sure I'd ever have another dog. Eventually I came round to the idea and researched different breeds, trying to find a working dog with a little less energy. Finally I settled on a beautiful blue merle collie.

Flora herds the animals, but unlike the Aussies, she also enjoys life in repose. My Perry Como dog. A loyal, friendly beast with a huge coat. But at fourteen, she is getting old, as dogs do, and dementia is setting in. I've been in denial about it and have been coping with her confusion, her wandering away and getting lost, her look of misery. It's been more than a year that I've known I'll have to do something. She disappeared in March, and it took more than twenty-four hours to find her stuck up to her withers in snow at the next farm. She's survived that and lags along pitifully until I finally break down and call for advice. I don't get past the fourth item on my list of ten concerns before the vet persuades me to bring her in. Flora's time has come.

As she aged, it was as if Flora's dementia, her loss of condition and energy prefigured mine. She became the embodiment of my future as I grow old. I haven't the heart to watch another dog fly through the years seven at a time. They all go so much faster now. I haven't energy for a puppy. Nor the desire to spend the hours necessary to train, clean up accidents, or deal with small animal veterinarians who now treat farm dogs as children and refer to their owners as Mum and Dad. Aging has left me dogless: too old to deal with a puppy, too raw to deal with an oldie.

Thankfully, I don't really need a dog for the flock. There are no large hills for sheep to hide behind, nor vast spaces to wander. At lambing, the ewes needn't be mustered; they stay near the barn. Later, to gather them from a paddock for treatment or sorting, I ring a vintage brass school bell. People say sheep are stupid, but Pavlov would be proud. One sound and they all come running; the young ones have no idea why, but being sheep, they follow. The older ewes, even the yearlings, can remember the taste of oats that follows the ringing. They almost knock me down in their exuberant rush to the feeders.

Hay is the only field crop we harvest. Because we have just one hayfield and sheep are picky eaters, the timing of the harvest is critical. We want it as young and tender as possible; we also want it dry. Early June is ideal for the crop but unpredictable for weather. A sudden strong shower on cut hay is disastrous. Not only does moisture toughen hay unpalatably, it can also overheat. Burn down a barn. We rely on our neighbour to custom cut and bale. And increasingly, as I age, to stack the bales in the barn. No longer am I strong enough to pack them tight, nor nimble enough to negotiate the barn beams.

Before we start haying, we must move the fleece. The sorting table, covered with bagged, tagged, and priced fleeces since they were shorn in March, is in the way. We sell all our wool privately, all that I don't spin and weave and knit myself. For years, a nearby philosopher had a wool company and bought from us, profit-sharing a decent price. He had a cottage industry of knitters; his wife designed the patterns. He could be found in the lotus position when we delivered our crop.

His circumstances changed and he could no longer buy wool, so we had to find a new market. We sent one year's shear to the main wool co-op and received not only a pittance but an insult. Since then, we have nurtured our own market. Spinners come to buy from us directly at the farm gate, and we take the remaining fleeces to a spinning seminar in June. In the past few years, we've sold out. There is immense satisfaction in having repeat customers, in pleasing people with our wool. Just before the hay is cut, we pack all the fleeces into the pickup and take them to the sale. The sorting table is turned on its edge and put against the far wall, the sawhorses are folded and put away, and the mow is empty, ready to receive the new crop of hay.

Lambsquarters lingers long in the last century with our use of small square bales. The hay is thrown by the baler into wagons but must be unloaded one by one onto the elevator, then stacked individually in the mow. Hot, heavy work. And work that requires skill.

All winter, we must take the hay down, bale by bale, and feed it out. When the mow is full, the hay rises to the rafters. Hand-hewn rungs form a ladder between two upright beams, and I climb it gingerly, happiest when the hay level falls below the highest crossbeam. But as we step back, our hay is more often stacked by a generation unfamiliar, and possibly disdainful, of our prehistoric methods. It gets stacked all in a flurry, all which-way. Loose here, tight there, the rows neglecting to follow the age-old pattern of alternate perpendicular layers. The front wall, open to the eye, must be perfectly plumb, perfectly alternate, perfectly tight. It holds the entire load. I should be able to climb to the top and work down through the layers, evenly unstacking from the summit row by row in an even plateau.

But no longer. The weather threatens rain; the workers stress for time. The mow is disorganized, treacherous in its instability. I've had one fall in the past from a badly built area. It broke my glasses and abraded my face. So I'm not risking trips up to the top this year.

Instead I'll use a long-handled cultivator, reach up as far as I can, and pull hard to get a bale down. It won't take long to work my way into the stack as one good pull tends to bring a bundle of bales each time. The trick is to stand back and not get pummelled by hay or the tool itself. It's effective, if not aesthetic. Instead of a nicely tuned hay mow, lowering course by course, I have a moth-eaten mess of domino bales.

The farm workers are young, inexperienced with our outmoded ways. But we are old, less nimble in the ways of mow-climbing, balancing, adapting. The hay gets stacked and no one is injured. This sure-footedness of youth eludes me. Frailty encroaches.

※.※

My father was born in June. And he died in June. He started out on Saint-Jean-Baptiste Day and breathed his last, almost ninety-two years later, on Bloomsday. Celebrations both. He was ready to die, and I witnessed his last breath.

For his eightieth birthday, my mother asked us to find him a tractor. He'd never owned one but had spent summers on his grandfather's farm, though likely, now I think of it, before the tractor's heyday. He did know horses. The farm team, and also the nag pulling the milk wagon he drove when he flunked out of law school.

His father's ultimatum was to go back to university or get out of the house. So in the late 1930s, he took off to Chicago, where he had a friend from his summers in Muskoka. His lifelong love of motors connected him with this wealthy American dairy magnate who collected and raced beautiful handcrafted wooden boats, many of them named for letters in the Greek alphabet. When Britain declared war, my dad immediately joined the Royal Air Force, no doubt leery of his future as a milkman. From boats to milk floats to planes, he became a pilot in the Royal Canadian Air Force, his affiliation switched when a week later Canada followed Britain into the fray.

Like most military pilots, he stopped flying after the war, though he often mused about having a float plane. He showed me where he would bunk this imaginary craft in a small inlet between rocky outcrops on the pristine northern Ontario lake where since his childhood he travelled each summer from the city to his family holiday cottage. When they retired from the city, my parents built a house on that lake on land inherited from my grandfather, and my father spent most of his time in the bush. He cut and split enough firewood to last several winters, despite the fact that they wintered elsewhere. He loved tramping in the bush, but though he sometimes talked about a plane, what he really wanted was a tractor. He wanted to make logging roads into the woods, and he wanted to drag logs along them. He wanted to clean up deadfall. Practise bush hygiene.

It wasn't difficult for me to find him a tractor. Farm country near me abounds in trade-ins. A 1952 Ford 8N appeared at the roadside with a For Sale sign, and a deal was made. Two thousand dollars. A red-belly Ford. You can still find them for two thousand dollars.

My dad spent many great years with this tractor and might have had more if my mother's health hadn't necessitated a move to town. When the time came, he offered it to me.

At first I had little use for it. I wasn't about to acquire the one-furrow plough implement featured in the manual, pictured with a farmer in grey flannel trousers and a fedora. We do use the scraper blade for grading the gravel lane, and there are lots of chains if we happen to have logs to pull. But when the first June of the millennium came, and I had my first significant income from writing my first book, I spent a bit of it on a rough-cut mower. It's a large rotary mowing attachment that runs off the power takeoff and is perfect for trimming pastures. By keeping the grasses from going to seed, nutrients continue to feed the plants, which continue to feed the sheep. So after each paddock rotation, I mow the grazed section and let it regrow until the next ovine visit.

My father was one of those macho guys who had to do everything himself. He was a lousy teacher, making me pull over, for instance, the only time he took me for a driving lesson. He was also terrified I'd get hurt. Losing his first-born child from illness made him overly protective. His hovering instilled in me a lasting fear of the danger of mechanical equipment. I was never allowed to have or ride a bicycle — which he considered lethal on the road — or anything else that he determined might be dangerous. He was always the one who drove, ran the boat, operated any machinery. This irrational fear made me anxious about equipment, and I was wary of this old tractor with its sticky clutch and open belts. He counselled that adding a mower only increased the odds of my being injured.

Calvin, from the farm equipment store, stemmed my fears. He delivered the mower and spent the whole afternoon teaching me about the tractor. He didn't just tell me: he got me on it and carefully and slowly took me through all the controls and possible scenarios. He hadn't an ounce of misogyny or disdain. He treated me like a farmer, not like some silly woman with an antique piece of junk. Now I could ride for hours up on that bouncing metal tractor seat, arms wide around the massive stiff steering wheel, stopping at a hill to shift to a lower gear that had no synchromesh, pushing up the throttle for the flat bits of the field. There's freedom in driving an open tractor. Even a small old Ford 8N. I felt a part of something greater. Some initiation into the history of farming, some sense of credibility, of belonging.

When my father died, we had a celebration of his life. Before people arrived at the farm, I cut a wide swath of the meadow with the tractor and mower for a parking lot. Instead of putting it away, I left the tractor out in the barnyard and attached my dad's work-boots to it, on either side, facing backwards. I'm not sure anyone noticed my gesture, but I'm fairly certain he'd have approved. We set up an easel with his first driver's licence and photos of him racing boats, flying planes, and one of him cutting the field with my mower, long after he'd given me the tractor. He'd grumbled when I made him wear ear protection (for the first time in his life), but his grin is enormous on that last drive.

He requested no ceremony and wanted his ashes left at the funeral home. He'd done the same with my sister Susan all those years ago, and it had always troubled me. She had leukaemia, died at five.

Susan was never spoken of, and when as an adult I asked about her burial, I was told there had not been one. They had left the ashes behind. There was a private memorial service and a death notice in the paper. That was it. My mother was pregnant with me at the time. Perhaps it was all she could manage.

After a long search, I discovered that — unbeknown to my mother — my father had signed a document to have Susan's remains buried in a common unmarked grave. I eventually hunted down the site, visited it, and imagined the box or urn of her ashes interred with many others in a known but unacknowledged spot in a grave-yard. I was not allowed to place a marker, so instead I surreptitiously planted bulbs to leave an offering. An acknowledgement that she had lived and that I would love to have known her.

So when my father died, I found it impossible to follow his instructions to abandon his ashes. You no longer own your body after death. The ashes came in a plain black plastic box. I decanted a few and placed them in a small metal canister for the glovebox of my car. He always loved a drive. A bit of him goes with me on outings, symbolically at least. The rest went onto his workbench, which is now in my basement. Among his beloved tools.

Then one June, we had the chance to go to my ancestral origin in Scotland. A cousin put me in touch with a Scottish historian, David Taylor, who had researched the six families who emigrated together from Badenoch in Inverness-shire to Canada in the early 1800s. He kindly agreed to meet us and take us to the exact place my forebears left behind. The McLean homestead dwellings are all gone, but the fields remain, beautifully wild, at the foot of the Cairngorms. We hiked in through woods and along streams, past ruins of drystone walls and grain-drying huts. While Thomas and David were deep in conversation, I wandered off alone, took out my folded map, and opened it to where I had stashed a few of my father's ashes. I'd been nervous of telling anyone I had them. Concerned that they'd look suspicious at customs — this bit of powder. And I wasn't sure of the legality of travelling with human remains. I know he wanted them left behind, but I felt a need to honour what was left of him in some way. Unlike Antigone, who sprinkled sand on the body, I dusted the sand with a sprinkling of the body.

As I age, I am clearing things away, trying to spare those who remain behind from having to dispose of a lifetime's acquisitions. It was time to find a final place for the rest of the ashes. June again, and back at the lake where my children have now inherited the property with the phantom-float-plane mooring, my daughter and I paddle out to disperse the ashes in the setting he loved best. I have no thought as to precisely where. It doesn't seem right to empty them in front of his house, now owned by another, or at my grandparents' summer cottage belonging now to a cousin. We paddle far into the lake, then return, hugging the shore. The float-plane inlet appears as we glide around the point, and I realize it is exactly right.

Still water reveals sparkling sand on the shallow bottom. Granite slopes covered with lichen line the sides, lush with leaning brush sheltering pines, maples, and birch. As I open the box and let the ashes drift over the side of the canoe, they form a silver thread drifting down through the water, mirroring the sun like mica. They continue in a stream as my daughter paddles up one side of the inlet, turns along the edge, and down the other side. At the mouth of the harbour, the box is empty.

❀ ❀

I spend much of June standing still. The month displays the fecundity of spring with new growth, new beings all around. If I walk softly, I observe them. The sheep go to the pie-shaped field in June, the farthest paddock from the buildings, so the one at most risk of predation. Coyotes howl in the night, and in June their whelps yip and sing. It makes me nervous to hear them, having lost lambs over the years. They rarely approach the farmstead, so every night I bring the flock into the chute behind the driveshed and close the gate behind them. In the morning, I walk back down, open the gate, and let them graze the pie-shaped field for another day until the rotation brings them back to closer paddocks.

The fox den I'd been watching across the road has relocated to the home farm. Just at the gate between the pie-shaped field and the hayfield, the vixen has enlarged an old groundhog hole and moved in her brood. Now I know why I'm not seeing them on my morning walk across the way. I recognize these two kits — one bold and brazen, the other timid with a good self-protective instinct. The first morning, I spot them undetected. They sit sunning themselves, stretching out, wrapping their tails around their bodies. Unlike their mother, who is thin and scruffy, they are pristine. Red bodies, black legs, full brushes of tails. Their foxy snouts point into the wind; their ears prick at the slightest sound.

The bold kit spots me the next day. It leaves its sentinel stone perch and walks toward me along the edge of the cedar wood. It stops, runs back, returns. I see it in silhouette, stark in the morning shade among the tree trunks, the open field in full sun behind. It looks over. I'm very still, but we've locked eyes. It knows I'm here. A litter mate, apparently alarmed, scurries down into the den, and I don't see it again that day.

Now each morning, and some evenings, I stand very still in the woods after I gather the flock. Almost always I'm awarded a sighting. Always it's thrilling. Playful wild animals sharing this property, keeping the mice and rabbits down, so far causing me no harm.

On my morning walk, I continue to see tracks but only in very wet or very dry spots. Raccoons kick up dust along the field edge, leaving their distinctive hand-like prints, and deer hooves sink into muddy bits near the water. A few times, the raccoon hasn't seen me coming as she forages in the bean field. Once she does, she's off lumbering awkwardly back into the woods. The deer, whose tracks seem seconds ahead of me on the path, hide expertly but for once when I am downwind. Like the raccoon, a doe is feasting on tender new bean plants as I stand rock-still watching. She grazes, then lifts her head, pricks her ears, looks around. Then grazes, pricks, looks. I don't know if she senses my presence, or if this is common twitchy behaviour. If deer cannot risk to relax.

I back up very slowly, and instead of continuing toward my usual trail, I enter the path through the poplars, which tremble above. When I return to the track, I peer out behind a cedar to find her still there, still eating, still vigilant. I pull back out of sight and set my camera, but by the time I look again, she is gone. No trace. I expect she watches me almost daily, but this is my only sighting of her this year.

A few days later, coming out of the woods onto the plateau, where I've planted a secluded field of wildflowers — my giardino segreto — a fawn suddenly runs out of the trees just a few metres away. Still in spots, its coat bright as a conker, its ears enormous, its legs gangly, it looks perplexed, frightened, confused. I stop, turn, hesitate. I hold my breath, a tree. I expect it to disappear, an apparition, a wish. Instead, the fawn runs toward me. I could touch it as it passes; then once again it stops. Bewildered, wild-eyed, dancing indecision. Then, like its mother, it bounds into the woods and vanishes.

How much am I not seeing? What subterranean rodents and furry mammals are living hidden on the farm? The skunk who grubbed the fields in early spring surely has a brood tucked away by June. The mice, the moles, the voles. Red, grey, and flying squirrels. Raccoons. Their tracks give them away, but I get just a glimpse.

Again, on the poplar path, something scurrying in the understory. It is a baby raccoon, giving itself away as it shinnies up a tree. Stock-still, tharn in camouflage, black and grey blending into bark. Except I see it climb. Focusing, I suddenly see another on a different tree. And then another. As I get out my camera, I spot a fourth on the tree beside me, level with my eyes. A breath away. It is absolutely frozen, barely breathing. There are six, all in different poplars, all completely still. Most face forward, but one looks out at me, her black mask shining in the dappled light. Not moving. As if they are highly trained guerrillas, experts in stealth, acting as one, a silent paralyzed team.

They are called "trash pandas" in the city. Pests who raid wheelie bins and wander busy neighbourhoods at night. They nest in chimneys and garages and generally make a nuisance of themselves. They've invaded my barn and my chimney in the past, and I've dispatched many over the years one way or another. I've seen them nest in hollow trees and hay mows, and they make a mess when they get into the stable. But I'd never before seen them hide in plain sight. And I wonder how many times I have walked right past them, unaware. And I wonder how many of these animals would make themselves scarce if I had a dog. What I've lost in domesticated companionship, I've gained in wild connection.

July

The birds are anting. Crouching down on anthills, nestling in, and spreading their feathers like hens covering their chicks. They waggle their tails as their wings shade the earth on the hottest days of summer. When all I want is to get out of the sun and away from the bugs, the robins and blue jays — like mad dogs and Englishmen — choose the hottest, driest places on the farm. Why they attract insects is unclear. Some speculate they use the ants to cleanse their feathers, or to soothe their bodies during moult. Insect valets. Others suggest that formic acid from the ants discourages lice and mites on the birds. Or perhaps by ridding the ants of their poison, the birds detoxify them to create a palatable snack.

Whatever the reason, the birds spend the first few days of July looking bizarre, as if digging into the lawn or spreading out after injury. Greenwood also spreads herself out, exposing as much of her body to the air as possible, but like me, she does this in the shade. It's too hot to work. The sheep take shelter under the cedars and put off grazing until late in the day.

Climate change makes our weather intense and unpredictable. The rains of June, typically making haying difficult to schedule, never arrive this year, and July is approaching full-on drought. The forecasts continue to promise rain in the near future, but it fails to appear. The sheep troughs need filling multiple times during the day; the grass turns brown; the garden shrivels. Humidity pushes the heat into the 40°C range.

I've never tolerated humidity well, and age isn't helping. The heat makes me feel sick, knots my stomach and joints, and keeps me from work. The reflective sunbaked garden ground wilts me as I try to weed and harvest limp lettuce and arugula. And early morning and late evening, while cooler, abound with black flies and mosquitoes. The summer we wait for all year turns on us, threatening to kill the plants, stress the sheep, desiccate the pastures.

I'd think it was the new normal, but last year was the opposite. So wet that the sheep suffered from relentless parasites that thrive on moist grass: Haemonchus (called barber pole worms for their red and white stripes), round worms, and tape worms. We were forced to treat them with anthelmintics and crutch the wool from their backsides to prevent fly-strike. The worms are increasingly resistant to drugs, so we are judicious in our application. Like bacteria, they mutate to avoid destruction, and like antibiotics, wormers have been overused and abused.

The new normal with climate change is no normal. Every year, every season, is unpredictable. It is difficult to prepare. And difficult to discuss with many who remember specific years of drought, years of flood, years of storms and stillness, but won't acknowledge their increasing frequency and intensity. Those who don't want to believe that we have done this to the Earth. To ourselves, to our offspring and theirs. The older I am, the more I recall difficult seasons, but they concertina in memory, making current weather seem familiar, when it clearly is not. All the climatic events of a lifetime are happening in high-speed sequence as the oceans and temperatures continue to rise and heads sink further and further into the sand.

City visitors seem unaware of the drought, happy to have hot holiday time, content to swim and tan and barbecue. They are surprised at our concern, not connecting the weather with the food they eat, not realizing the crops they see out the car window will eventually be on their grocery shelves, morphed beyond recognition. Hay feeds the beef and lamb on their tables. Corn fattens chickens and pigs. Wheat makes their bread. Farmers feed cities. But so many are disconnected from the source, inexperienced with what grows on trees, what underground. And with so much factory farming, there are fewer and fewer animals on pasture to remind those driving by. A Holstein cow is a rare sight in a field these days, though there are close to a million of them in the country, packed into barns, many milked by robots.

As well as anting birds, July brings flocks of new hatchlings. Baby robins fledge from a nest in the driveshed, oddly perched on the back carrier of my daughter's old bicycle hanging from the rafters. Four speckled fluffballs take off in sequence on their first flight, landing on various pieces of machinery until they make it outside into the world. Rose-breasted grosbeaks bring their young to the feeders, the males brown and striped like their mothers but with orange chest feathers heralding the crimson to come. Downy woodpeckers feed chicks as big as themselves but less clever; I see one pecking diligently at the concrete post of the bird bath. Bluebirds seem to be feeding young, until they stop, and I check to see the nest empty of either eggs or chicks. Something must have attacked, but with a secure opening and a protective screen at the entrance, the only predator that might have entered is a snake. The birds are still around. Perhaps they'll try again.

Because of climate change and farming practices, there are birds I no longer see. Hawks were frequent residents in the past. Red-tailed and sparrowhawks particularly, as well as harriers, rough-legged hawks, sharp-shinned, and even the occasional peregrine falcon. They've been replaced by turkey vultures, who circle high over the fields, detecting death and decomposition. Large ugly birds, useful for cleaning up carrion but lacking the nobility of the raptors. Pheasants too have largely disappeared, with the bobolinks and meadowlarks. The hummingbirds have sadly dwindled. Food sources have changed, nesting sites have disappeared, and pesticides have flourished. Starlings, grackles, crows, and ravens adapt. Robins, chickadees, and goldfinches abound. So far.

Between haying and harvest, there is a little lull. Festivals fill in the space, and locally it's the sheep shearing competition. Just down the road, tents are set up in a large farm field, food booths appear, and chairs are unstacked in front of the raised three-stand shearing platform. Gates and pens hold hundreds of heavy lambs ready to be shorn as the shearers sharpen their gear and don their singlets to compete. Judges in white lab coats skitter across the board to inspect the shearers as they work, assigning demerit points for wool left on the animal. Rousies whisk the wool away, and timers sit with stopwatches, thumbs poised. Shearers are mostly men, though this year it is a woman who wins the speed competition. She isn't actually the fastest in her class, but she is the most careful; the speed demon she beats is disqualified for flaws in his work.

The contest attracts shearers from as far away as Australia and as close as a few kilometres. They work together, even as they compete, helping to load the sheep in and out of the pens, catching the odd escapee who pitches into the chute prematurely — or more spectacularly into the audience — providing commentary and encouragement. The prize money is significant, and they push themselves to win it, shearing as many as twenty sheep in speedy succession. Our shearer demonstrates blindfolded and releases a perfectly shorn animal in less than a minute.

Thomas and I started off as rousies, gathering wool from the board as it comes off the sheep, piling it into baskets, then running with it to bales set up for holding fleece. It was punishing work crouching down so the audience could see the shearers, then jumping up to rake in the wool, down again, then all the way up and running. It happens so quickly there is no chance for a rest. It's nothing compared to what the shearers are doing, but they are young, incredibly fit, determined. After a number of years, we had to relinquish the job. I found my quads just couldn't take it anymore, and now we sit on chairs with stopwatches and mark time.

The July after my father died, after the hay went into the barn, I decided to clear out the straw mow. It was almost empty, but before the new crop came in, I wanted to get right down to the bare floor, sweep it clean, dispose of any old rotten bales. Once that was done, I started to think about the granary. It is a wooden cube structure built on one side of the hayloft, taking up about a quarter of the space and positioned south of centre. Nine feet high with a flat ceiling and roof, its upper surface was covered with the ancient hay bales and animal droppings we'd bought with the farm.

In a clearing mood, I determined to haul it all away. I had no plan for the new space; I just wanted it clean. Many Gator trips later, we got down to bare wood. Rotting bare wood.

The view from the top is fetching. Fresh-cut hay bales across the mow, sun filtering through the slats of barnboard, polished hand-hewn rungs shining from years of boot steps on the vertical ladder leading to the top of the straw. As soon as it was swept off, I knew it was a space that had to be used. Captured.

My first thought was a stage. A string quartet playing to an audience below. Beethoven's C-sharp minor perhaps. A stellar idea but not an enduring endeavour, so I imagined some variant of a childhood fort up there. Somewhere I could go to write, or think, or produce. A prefabricated wooden structure or shed perhaps. But that would block the view. It needed to be something transparent, like the crystalline church in *Oscar and Lucinda*. Something I could see through. Somewhere new for me to weave.

My loom, once the pride of my house loft, got pushed farther and farther into a corner as my writing and artistic lives increasingly colonized the space. It was crowded out by multiplying bookshelves and filing cabinets, painting tables, easels, and art supplies. The wool baskets leaned forlornly against the wall, the loom pushed out of the way. I had to move everything to use it. So I rarely did. Work on my desk glared at me if I wove. Half-finished paintings flashed their empty white space. I needed somewhere away from other duties, away from the household chores. A space apart and yet connected.

A glass house. Perched inside the barn on top of the granary. A woollen grow op. To craft fabric and clothing, scarves and blankets. To turn the fleece from below into fine woollen goods within the sound of the sheep who provide it. We had an old door in the driveshed made of eight large panes of glass and our carpenter fit it sideways into the barn wall, opening the view to the west. A greenhouse maker in the Holland Marsh agreed to supply and set up the structure, and I had a small legacy from my grandfather's estate, something my father had neglected to sort out before he died.

When the workers arrived, on the hottest of hot July days, they were surprised at the location. Flummoxed. Never before had they installed a glass house inside a building. Or up on a platform. I spent the day bringing lemonade and apologizing, hoping they would someday be able to dine out on the story of this bizarre farmer who wanted a greenhouse inside her barn. Piece by piece, they assembled glass panes and peaked roof until a marvellous crystal palace appeared, the sun glinting through, the view from within panoramic. As my grandfather had been an officer in the wars, I call it the Colonel's Crystal Palace.

I have rattan window blinds for glaring July afternoons and a micro furnace for late fall and early spring. There are lights; there can be music. It's so far up that visitors often don't see it when they come to the mow. Not everyone is invited for a closer look. It's an aerie. A perch to view the sheep in distant paddocks; a pellucid capsule bounded by hay and straw and barn. I am level with Greenwood, curled up on top of the hay mow after a night of carousing; we're out of sight of everyone else.

Initially I climbed the perpendicular ladder and swung myself around onto the platform to the greenhouse door. But when the fresh straw was depleted by the next July, and the new crop not yet in, Thomas built me a stairway made of haybales so I could walk up alongside the granary wall. They sufficed for a few years but deteriorated and became dangerous, their binder twine sticking up and threatening to trip me as the hay packed down. New bales would be fine, but when some outside work was needed on the barn, Thomas insisted on having the carpenter build a proper wooden staircase. It's easier, but it's a visual reminder of my age, my impending infirmity.

Although acquired in July, the crystal palace sees little action this month. It's too hot to work with wool, and there's too much to do elsewhere on the farm. The raspberry bushes must be tied and tidied; the peas need daily picking, podding, freezing; weeds invade the delphiniums and lupins. The days are long and full, beginning with the flock, who must be counted and accounted for, examined, watered, and frequently moved.

This year, we've changed the fence configuration. Previously, the meadow field was divided into three sections descending away from house westward, the temporary fences running north and south. The animals gained access to the different sections through small gates from the chute at the north side, the original farm track. They had to made a sharp left turn to get there and invariably the new-crop lambs would be stymied and run frantically back up to the barnyard as their mothers disappeared into the field. Or they'd see their mothers but not the access and bash themselves into the wire fence trying to get through. Sheep prefer to follow a curved pathway or enter a wide opening. This setup was never easy for any of us.

Watering too was tricky. Large rubber troughs had to be moved with every paddock change, and water delivered by gravity feed from a tank on the back of the Gator. It took a long time to fill it from the hose at the barn and even longer to empty. I took a book.

The sheep love the top section, near the house, and seem to hate to be at the middle or the bottom. Whenever we leave the farm for someone else to look after, we put the flock at the top for convenience, and frequently the grass there is overgrazed. Brilliantly, this year Thomas set the fences up in the opposite direction, with four separate parallel strips all running from the top section to the bottom. Now the sheep can spend time near the house, but because the segments are smaller they're more inclined to graze the grasses at the bottom of each section. They sleep by the house each night, away from the woods and the coyotes. Now the water bowls can be moved along the rail fence by the house and filled in each paddock with a garden hose. The fences are easily opened at the top, and the flock learns instantly where to go next.

They also seem to be able to count: they begin to complain vocally after five days in one section. Move us, move us, they seem to say. Standing by the edge of the next greener section, they look back at me over their shoulders. Move us.

So far this year, the hot dry weather has spared us a deluge of parasites. And without the scourge of daggy backsides, we've seen no fly-strike. Ever vigilant, I'm constantly on the lookout for a scratching animal or one biting at its flank. A patch of wet or dirty wool is a warning sign that flies might have invaded. Every shepherd has seen fly-strike, and none of us ever wants to see it again. Countless eggs are laid on the affected area, and seething swarms of maggots mill and roil over the skin, feeding on flesh. If we catch it soon enough, we can get it under control, kill the maggots, and treat the wound. If left too long, the flies win and the lamb dies. In any case, it must be a horrific experience for the animal; it's horrific enough for the shepherd.

The dry weather means day after day of walling for Thomas. He's out at first light, needs to be coaxed back for morning coffee, then lunch on the verandah, his clothes too filthy to go inside. He wears steel-toed Australian boots, trousers with thick double knees which still manage to wear out with all the rough granite they hoist, prescription safety glasses. He slathers himself in sunscreen, neglecting to spread it out and smears of white compete with dirt where he's wiped away the sweat or swatted a bug. I treasure these times sitting together for a break in the late morning or lunch in a hot noon sun, the breeze wafting through the lilacs, spent now but filled with chickadees and finches chattering away, flitting to the feeders, brushing against my hat, landing on my hand.

Thomas relates a specific rock from his morning, its recalcitrance or its plasticity. The ones that refuse to fit; the ones that find a perfect spot. We talk of our time on Shetland where we boldly knocked on the door of a drystone dyker — Tom Jamieson — and asked to talk trade. He invited us in, made tea, served biscuits, showed us pictures of his walls, talked of his work. I had found his address in the yellow pages, and we knew we were in the right place when we saw his truck outside, the familiar stone chisels and hammers in the back. He could not have been more friendly, and we could not have been more grateful to meet such a man. But it went on. He arranged to meet us the following day and drove us all over mainland Shetland to show us almost every wall he'd ever built and projects he was working on at the time.

There were commercial walls and private walls, parkland walls, and even a memorial wall. He'd made a geological wall with all the varied types of stone on the island: stone arches, angled corners, coped tops, diagonal courses. There were red walls, pink walls, grey walls, and walls black with age that he repaired. His hospitality was rich, his language a gift. An inspiration.

SOMETIMES A STONE

Sometimes a stone just walks into place
Says Tom, rock-dyker Shetland man,
Walling on at a simmer dim pace.

He sets batter at every wall's base,
Laid wide for the vertical plan:
Sometimes a stone just walks into place.

His persistence forms rock into grace
Where ratchie nor riebeckite scan,
Walling on at a simmer dim pace.

Stone nails slim shim into slopes and space
From Flagna Field, Hadd, or Heogan:
Sometimes a stone just walks into place.

A wee gate redeems in unlikely case
Of rocks not coping to span,
Walling on at a simmer dim pace.

He needs no sign to leave his trace,
His hearting and course name the man.
Sometimes a stone just walks into place
Walling on at a simmer dim pace.

August

ugust is a month of spiders and storms. Webs appear as tiny hammocks suspended from cedars or grass stalks. Cup-shaped parlours, or grids with zippered centres connecting raspberry bushes, they invite insects in for a treacherous nap in silk. Tiny arachnids share household corners with delicate daddy-long-legs. I've been told one is never more than a metre away from a spider. In August, the distance seems to shrink.

When hot, humid days keep warm air near the ground and cool air hovers above, lightning strikes and thunder cracks. The power fails. We take cover. For much of this August, the sheep, uncharacteristically, are being sheltered. The endless days of humidity paired with cooler nights mean more moisture on the grass, more flies in the air.

For the first time, we have an outbreak of pink eye — keratoconjunctivitis — a bacterial infection. I've never see it before and am baffled when I find Clemmie, a lovely young ewe, completely blind, stumbling in the field, frantically trying to find the rest of the flock. I can see right away that her eyes are clouded over — bluish, pinkish. The diagnosis is easy to make when I realize that others have exudate around their eyes. And flies, scads of flies. As more animals are affected, I bring the flock into the barn and spend much of the month trying to get the disease under control.

My research suggests that though highly contagious, pink eye must begin with an infected sheep. As I have a closed flock, with no new animal introduced for a number of years, where did it come from? The veterinarian says flies. There are other sheep now grazing a farm close by. I hear them baaing sometimes on my walk, and at first I worried that mine had escaped. Perhaps the infection comes from there. Perhaps not. In any case, flies have brought it to Lambsquarters and we are all suffering.

I begin by separating the afflicted and bringing them into the barn. I disinfect water bowls and salt feeders. With baby shampoo, I wash the infected eyes and put in drops three times each day. Clemmie, the first and by far the worst, is given systemic antibiotics; within a week, she can see and appears to be clear of disease. Others also improve, but those left on pasture begin to show signs of infection. After days of bringing the flock in each day and separating the sick, I finally give up and bring everyone into the barn. So when the worst thunderstorm of the season comes close and knocks the power out, the sheep are safely under cover.

A previous year, we'd not been so fortunate. The sheep were pasturing in the pie-shaped field. The bottom of the lane at the so-called bee yard is lined in cedars, a favourite shady spot for ruminating on a hot August day when they're in that paddock. I was in the house when a sudden storm blew up, trying to calm our then-young collie Flora, who quivered at the thunder crashes. It wasn't a particularly long or fierce storm, though it clearly was very close. The power stayed on.

Late that afternoon, the sun shining again and Flora settled, we went out to bring the flock in-bye for the night. Most of them came when I opened the gate, but I could see some lagging behind, lying down in a row in their favourite cool spot. I called to them; no response.

Flora and I walked down to get them. All too soon it became clear that they would not be coming to the barnyard that night. Pressing against one of the trees was a beautiful black lamb. Behind her, in a queue, were five other ewes, all touching, the last in the line lying with a hind foot stretched out.

They were all dead.

The cedar had been hit; the lightning travelled down the trunk, through one sheep after another and finally out to ground through the last hind leg. Carnage.

Home alone, I was unsure what to do. A neighbour suggested I call my insurance agent, as livestock are covered under the farm policy, and said I'd need photographs and a veterinarian to certify the cause of death. A livestock coroner. I began with the insurance company, and as it was after hours, I reached someone far away, not my familiar local agent. She was overwhelmingly helpful and kind.

"Are you all right?" she asked.

It hadn't occurred to me to consider my emotional state. It was devastating, but it was livestock, not a disaster in the house. One toughens somewhat after years of farming. Her question, however, brought me back to the level of loss. All those animals

I had bred and delivered, had nurtured as part of a breeding programme, part of an overall plan. I knew them all so well, had such hopes for their future contribution to the flock. "Should I take photographs?"

"Do you think you can?" she asked, as if revisiting the scene would be painful.

I never needed the photographs, nor the veterinarian. The insurance company not only covered the value of the animals, they actually gave extra for their burial.

At the time, Canada was undergoing a problem with BSE, bovine spongiform encephalopathy, commonly known as mad cow disease. Because it is similar to a prion protein disease that can occur in sheep, dead stock dealers refused to pick up sheep carcasses. We had to bury them ourselves.

Over the years, many animals have found graves on the farm. An aging ewe, a still-born lamb, a succession of dogs and barn cats. Holes have been dug; animals have been committed. But six? All at once? The only solution was to dig a mass grave with the tractor, place the beasts into the front-end loader a couple at a time, and tip them with care into the hole. Nothing could make this palatable. No matter how gently we lifted them onto the tractor, desperately heavy in their dead weight, no matter how slowly the loader tipped them out. It was a deep hole in the ground with six lifeless woolly animals gone for good.

I tossed in flowers. Stupidly, I suppose, but with a need to acknowledge the gravity of the event, the extent of the loss I felt. Feel still. Thomas covered them over, packed down the earth, planted fresh seed overtop. There is no marker, of course, but I know where they are and think of them in the summer shade of their quiet place on the farm.

So far this August, we've lost no lambs, no ewes. The season is not over, and I must not be complacent. I hear coyotes at night, yipping and yapping somewhere close, and I see their scat on my morning walks, sometimes with the remnants of a nighttime kill. A rodent, a rabbit. Parasites can still be a problem, and the odd ewe is still lactating, still vulnerable to the possibility of mastitis. Injury is around every corner, a sore foot, a stuck head, a cut flank. And fly-strike in this hot humid month. I must be ever wary. And still the eyes. Just when I think I have cured one animal, another presents with the infection. Clemmie continues to relapse, even to the point of blindness once again.

I hear desperate baaing one morning after the flock is back on pasture, and I find her at the top of the paddock, turning in frantic circles, bashing into the fence, ears back, eyes wild behind their clouded film. Back to the barn, more treatment, more worry. How will I ever get this under control? If only the hot, humid weather would break, sending the flies elsewhere.

In desperation, I try other methods. There's a blue spray some recommend, a mix of boric acid, urea, and gentian violet. The animals hate the sound of the spray, hate the feel of it as well, and treating becomes harder and harder as they begin to object to being caught and handled. I buy a pony-sized fly mask, altering it to fit a ewe. It velcros onto the animal and is effective for pasturing horses, but horses are used to bridles, bits, and breastplates.

A ewe, unaccustomed to apparel, is unlikely to appreciate being masked, unlikely to understand how it might help. So for the moment, it sits in a drawer.

My "barn nanny," the wonderful neighbour I hire to chore when I can't be here, has horses. Kathryn is energetic, conscientious, and vivacious. An expert in martial arts, a former school bus driver, a rural postie, she is always available to help me, always eager. Like so many horse people, she takes great pride in her stable, and I am always amazed at how clean and sparkling my barn is after she's chored in my absence. She even bought her own broom to use here. Biosecurity. She has learned enough about sheep to have my full confidence, whereas I know nothing about horses.

"What about fly spray?" she said.

"Fly spray?"

Turns out those equine fly masks aren't the whole picture. There is a fly repellant spray to mist or rub on the beasts' faces and spray on masks to keep insects away. How did I not know this? I will try anything to fight this continuing conjunctivitis.

By now, the sheep have had more than enough attention. I have no trouble enticing them into the barn with a few oats, but once there and crushed, it is our habit to section them off, a few at a time, with a portable hinged pen. I walk around behind them, and they go in the open end. Then Thomas quickly shuts them in to be treated. Only now they are reluctant to go anywhere near the pen. They're onto us. They're tired of having their eyes baby-shampooed. They don't want to be sprayed blue. And they likely don't want to smell of citronella either. Can't say I blame them.

Nonetheless, it must be done if we are to beat this thing. Down to the last animal, just after I finish applying the repellant with my right hand, she goes berserk, bashing herself against the pen. Unfortunately, I am holding onto the inside edge of the pen tightly with my gloved left hand, keeping me balanced as I lean in.

Sheep bunt to protect themselves or to sort a disagreement about their spot in the field, their place at a feeder. Usually they bunt with their heads down and forcefully connect with their poll, but the hard head can also bash sideways. I think this is what is happening. Tina, a large chocolate-brown-fleeced ewe, swings her bony head sideways into my bent hand and puts all her weight behind the thrust. It is all I could do to free myself and stamp away in pain, moaning, unsure of the extent of damage. It feels as if all my fingers are broken. I feel sick with the crushing pain, and only stomping and pacing around the now empty pen seem to soothe me. Eventually I am able to pull off the glove to find badly bruised, badly contused fingers. I rush to get my ring off and run cold water from the feed room tap on my swelling hand.

"Can you make a fist?" Thomas asks. And I can. Nothing broken, except blood vessels, which accounts for the exquisite pain.

I must now protect my hand and it will be some time before the bruises fade, but the worst is past. I should be able to put my ring back on soon.

Farming is dangerous business. Farm accidents account for five times the death rate of workers in other industries and have the greatest risk of injury causing disability. Most cases involve machinery. Animals, however, account for the next most likely cause of morbidity and mortality.

Sheep are rarely lethal. Compared to horses and cattle, sheep are small. My Border Leicester ewes weigh about 75 to 80 kilos; rams 110 kilos or more. Certainly they are strong enough to cause injury well beyond my battered fingers. They outweigh me and have a steadier stance with their four legs on the ground. Once I was knocked over in the barnyard when I was pregnant, and since then I've never turned my back on a ram. In fact, I rarely enter a pen with a ram. They have extremely hard polls and use their head to bunt when riled up. Usually it amounts to a knock on the knee, but it can result in a serious clipping injury. Best to keep my distance.

Farmers expect to be injured and tend not to report. Perhaps our embarrassment features, as well as our acceptance of the consequences of a dangerous working environment.

A cracked rib years earlier was a direct result of a lamb robustly kicking me in the chest. Since then, if I have to hold a lamb for Thomas to treat, I gently pick it up holding its hind legs between its forelegs, its back against my chest. With a good grip, I can keep it steady and calm and keep us all safe.

Frequently I find myself taking risks that could lead to injury and inevitably lead to bruises. I climb over fences rather than walk to the distant gate. I carry heavy feed bags or large bales that would be better left for my "hired man." I prop a manure fork against a feeder where it could fall and hurt me when I should hang it on its hook. I climb up an unsteady mow to throw down hay when I should use my cultivator, or I scramble up the vertical ladder instead of using the stairs.

These are all things I got away with in the past. When I was young and nimble, I could clear a fence with ease. Now my balance is off, my feet cramp, and I know I'm not as steady as I need to be. Aging on the farm is a detriment to safety. But I am not alone. As young people leave the farm and move to the city, remaining farmers get older. In the recent past, the number of farmers over eighty in Canada has increased by 58 percent, and the accidental death rate of these older farmers exceeds the national average by more than 40 percent. Everything is a little bit harder, a little bit slower, a little bit more difficult to remember with each year.

When I was a teenager, I spent a summer in Muskoka as a mother's helper for a cousin. My great uncle Philip was a pilot, who flew his amphibious plane every few days between the city airstrip where he worked and their summer home on a northern lake. He was an accomplished flyer, a gentle giant of a man. He had been a fighter pilot with the Royal Flying Corps over France in the First World War, was an instructor at an English flying school, barnstormed with legendary flying ace Billy Bishop, and later directed an aircraft company. He'd been flying to the cottage for over forty years without incident until one day that summer, in his seventies, he made a mistake. Stopping at a local airstrip to bring up the ladder that had been left unloaded at takeoff, he was distracted and neglected to follow through the rote landing checklist. Worried about hitting the water with the ladder hanging down below the level of the pontoons had taken his mind off the crucial preparation for landing on the lake just minutes later, and he forgot to raise the wheels into the pontoons. Instead of gliding along the water, the plane tipped forward on the wheels and quickly began to sink. My uncle and his passengers survived with a few cuts and scrapes. He never flew again. It's the short-term memory that goes first. The small details that count and can kill.

I make lists to go to the barn. I try to plan ahead, to anticipate accidents in order to prevent them. But animals are unpredictable. Even with years of studying sheep psychology — watching closely to learn where they are likely to move, how they will react — I am still frequently surprised. I take fewer chances, cut fewer corners, spend more time in preparation. I go through my checklist, then go through it again.

In an effort to stay nimble, I walk every day. The gardens and animals keep me moving, but activities vary with the weather and with the season. It's not always easy to get out there for more than the requisite chores. Many days I agree with Jane Eyre that there is "no possibility of taking a walk that day." But she had no Gore-Tex, and I have no excuse. Usually in the morning, before the chores, I head down the lane or along the field and into the woods.

Since my son-in-law motivated me to venture out each day, whatever the weather, I walk or ski, snowshoe or trudge, and take a photo and text it to him. It compels me to get off my window seat, put down my book, and face the day. It helps to keep me fit.

I travel a similar route daily, always stopping at the same spot to take and text my photo. There are optional side trails and varying directions, and I can choose the length of my journey. Often I'm in a rush and determine to go only as far as necessary, but once in stride I carry on — wondering if the stream will be rushing faster with the rain, if there will be a deer around the corner if I walk into the wind, if yesterday's mushrooms will have thrown spores or dissolved into a pool of black ink.

In August, the signs of autumn begin. The first traces of colour appear on reddening maples, yellowing poplars. Starlings begin to gather. Mushrooms sprout like illusions — growing riotously overnight. Reindeer moss, puffballs, shaggy manes, and fairy rings dance around the forest floor, changing places in do-si-dos from day to day. Mystery fungi brighten up the humus and punctuate the leaf mould in scarlet, chartreuse, vermilion, and ochre. Copious rain springs them to a valiant performance before the frost.

One side trail, up a hilly cedar bank, one day displays fallen apples. Little green apples, just a few, multiply into many over a week. I search high and low but can find no apple tree among the cedars. Nor do I see evidence of animals who might have placed them. They are unscratched, unbitten, unblemished, and there is no obvious scat. Day after day, I revisit the spot trying to understand. But not until I go much farther up the hill, into the meadow, and beyond the lane to the gate do I find the fruiting tree. Not only is it many metres from the apples, there is also a high berm in between. There is no explanation. All I can do is name the spot Appleyard and watch and wait to see if the apples are eaten. So much mystery in the woods.

Some of my walks take me into unaltered land — swamp too dense to traverse, too wet to plough, too rough to clear. I've no doubt it would have been passable to those First Peoples with such superior skills, but it took a great effort by Thomas and our son-in-law to create a path through. Over the course of the summer,

Thomas follows the flag-tape route they'd set out over a week-end's slog through the wooded bog. Painstakingly, he creates stone berms, cedar bridges, and elevated corduroy walkways in a serpentine pattern through hemlocks, cedars, poplars, and balsam; over patches of jewelweed, moss, watercress, and open water; alongside a stream, under a thick summer canopy, the sun filtering through in shades of lime and mint.

The materials for the bridges and berms all come from the ground they sit on, rearranged only. In early August, the water is high from the rain, the corduroy slick. Spotted jewelweed, *Impatiens capensis*, glows orange, its flower throats dotted in beguiling crimson, its seed pods ready to explode at the slightest softest impact, giving it the name touch-me-not. Treefrogs sing, camouflaged like lichen on old bark.

Leopard frogs leap from the swamp into the long meadow grass on the plateau, wet from heavy August dew, their brilliant green backs spotted, their bodies slim and sleek. Deer wander, fledging swallows line the wire to the barn, amorous ewes prance as they come into oestrus.

❀❦

Toward the end of the month, a momentous walk takes place. We are invited to join our neighbouring family in solemnly sowing the ashes along their forest floor of my great friend Maik, who befriended me as soon as I pitched up in this place. She taught me how to throw a bale of hay, how to pluck a chicken, how to make a life on the land. When my daughter was born, and Thomas was called away, she marched into the house, right up the stairs, and took care of me on that third night — the notorious time for hormonal surges that plague new mothers. She guided me through so many stages of learning how to farm and how to cope. She was the best neighbour imaginable.

The day dawns bright and verdant as we gather in the maple bush. With her large family (she was the oldest of ten), we walk slowly along the forest trails that she and Gerrit created, tended, and cherished. One by one, we are handed a silver spoon and invited to fill it carefully with her silver ashes and silently sprinkle them.

Maik arrived in Canada after floods devastated Holland in the 1950s. Her father had to cut a hole in the roof of their house so they could be rescued from the water rising in their attic. One of her much younger sisters told me Maik had dressed her in multiple layers that day, dress over dress, sweater over sweater, before their escape. Maik rarely spoke of it. She worked as hard as any farmer could without the advantage of modern equipment or the comforts of central heating, modern conveniences, or vacations. Every day, she and Gerrit milked the cows, morning and night, fed the calves, mucked out the pigs, drove the tractors, and nurtured their three kids, their grandchildren, and their great-grandchildren, who called her GG.

After Gerrit died, she sold the cows, rented out the fields, and dispersed the implements. But she kept her hens. Over fifty of them in loose housing in the barn, free run. Always she left a note on the kitchen table if she was away from the house, saying where she was and instructing her clients to help themselves to eggs from the fridge. She carried on into her eighties until she quietly died one night in her sleep. A sad day for us all, but a life lived well, with tenacity. What a privilege for us to share in her memorial, to walk with her in her woods one last time.

꽃.꽃

The garden, its walls growing daily through Thomas's current drystone art, begins to groan. Cobs of corn seem to ripen all at once, beans must be picked each day, and onions queue up on the stone wall to dry until I can find time to plait their stems for storage. I carry the harvests in large wicker baskets and fill the kitchen with the messes and scents of food being prepared for winter. Cauldrons of tomato sauce, batches of basil pesto, pots of raspberry jam, packets of beans and corn for the freezer. There is so much to do that meals must be quick and easy. In the morning, I set out lamb chops in a marinade of oil and lemon with thyme, marjoram, and rosemary I gather on my way in from chores. In the late afternoon, work done, I pick cherry tomatoes for a fast burst pasta sauce. While Thomas grills the chops, I add the whole tomatoes to a pan with a little olive oil. They soon gently explode into a delicious sweet slurry to top some penne or fusilli. Fresh basil in the sauce, parsley and mint to garnish the chops. A glass of wine. Then fresh berries.

The raspberries come from the pig garden, in front of the driveshed. Though we never warmed to pigs, they did an excellent job of rooting up their patch and I've grown raspberries on the fertile soil there ever since. My grandsons make a beeline there when they visit in August. I give them containers, but I know they eat more than they save. And I love to see them do it, remembering my own grandmother offering to bake a pie if I brought back enough wild blueberries during my childhood summers up north. I have no memory of a pie, just stained fingers and face.

It's not only vegetation harvest time. In August, we start marketing our lambs. This can be the most difficult part of farming. The philosophical arguments are difficult for me. Putting animals on the truck is difficult. Driving to the stockyards with lambs to sell, or to the abattoir with lambs for the freezer, is never, ever, an easy job. I much prefer to sell my animals as breeding stock, but it just isn't possible to sell them all. There are only so many rams anyone needs. As one tup can service forty or fifty ewes, few are required.

Most farmers in Canada keep sheep for meat. There are sheep dairy farms and elite flocks of purebred breeding stock, but like mine, they tend to be small operations. I have the advantage of excellent fleece quality from a relatively rare breed, so with my niche market I can sell my wool at a considerable premium. Commercial wool production in Canada is insignificant and unprofitable, so there is little incentive for most farmers to produce clean fleece or to breed for excellent wool. Lambs are routinely selected to achieve the best carcass quality in the shortest amount of time. Many lambs are marketed right off the grass, but there is a rising trend to pack them into feedlots, leg-of-lamb by mutton-chop, where they spend the rest of their lives confined, where the lights rarely go out, and where all they have to do is interact and eat. Only by anthropomorphizing can I make a judgment as to how the lambs feel. They can't tell me.

And perhaps it is my guilt at raising animals to be eaten that makes me believe my system is kinder for them. Really nothing can improve the reality.

We used to hire a drover to transport the animals, but some years ago we decided to do it ourselves. Thomas made a loading chute from our kids' old wooden playground equipment, the bright-yellow-painted slide is the ramp, now modified with horizontal slats. He also created stock racks for the pickup truck. They too are unsophisticated and include an old shutter from my grandparents' cottage as a door. When we pull up to the dock at the stockyards, we stand out against all the shiny pots, the proper livestock trailers.

Usually it is fairly easy to load the lambs. I might put in a few apples or tempt the first one with a bit of grain, and then they predictably follow like sheep. Occasionally we might have to use a shepherd's crook. These sometimes have a metal hook on one end, the curved wooden crook at the other. A sheep will be caught by hook or by crook.

It's a difficult day, no matter how easily it goes. But it's gratifying to produce a good product, to take pride in the work, and to look forward to the cheque later in the week. And mostly it is a relief to have it over and move on to the next stage of the year. After all the years I've been doing this, it has not become any better. It fills me with regret, year after year.

And yet I am an omnivore; I eat meat. I find it difficult to explain to those who don't, but I do take comfort in the fact that I treat the lambs from my farm as ethically and carefully as I can manage. I do not use medicated feed or artificial lighting or keep them in cramped spaces. I do not treat my ewes with hormones to force them to breed out of season. I do not operate a feedlot. I do not wean my lambs early.

There are local farms where lambs are brought in from other breeders and put into huge crowded pens to be fattened. But there are also large-scale sheep farms where the animals are kept outside. Some local sheep graze all summer between the rows of solar farms. Other grassland farmers keep their flocks outdoors all year long. They graze permanent pastures in the summer, move to planted grazing crops in the autumn, and eat feed delivered by tractors hauling bale rollers and snacker feeders onto the snow all winter.

My flock will stay on pasture a little longer, but August is the time to assess the ewes and decide which to keep, which to cull. We examine their mouths for soundness. They should have most of their eight incisors in the lower front jaw, and they cannot be too worn down. Sheep without teeth are called gummers, and they must go as they cannot graze properly. Ewes who have not bred or had enough milk to raise their lambs might also have to go. Sometimes I give them another chance if they are neophytes. It's a time of reflection. A time to analyze the season past and prepare for the one to come.

September

With most of the lambs sold, I'm relieved to be at less risk of predator danger. As autumn sets in, the coyotes howl at night, their hungry pups voicing high-pitched yelps from one patch of forest to another across the pastures. They too are preparing for colder weather; they need to fatten up. Ripening berries, windfall apples, and small mammals comprise most of their diet. But a lamb is a huge bonus. It is devastating to find a beautiful animal completely gutted lying dead in the field. And whenever it happens, I manage to find myself at fault. I should have brought them in sooner from the far fields at night, let them out later in the morning. I should have finished trimming the long grass in the pasture, not left cover for the coyote to stalk.

Colder weather in September affects the parasites and flies. Sometimes we have killing frosts as early as Labour Day, which depletes insects and sends the worms into dormancy. The remaining lambs are well weaned so mastitis is no longer a risk in the ewes. But this year, global warming firmly established, it is still unreasonably hot, sultry, humid. The flies abound. The pink eye problem persists. Sheep go through a revolving door between the barn and pasture as they recover and relapse, and I'm ready to give the whole thing up.

My hand is improving from August's crush injury, but a large black bruise remains on my ring finger, travelling like a lazy snail from somewhere under the injured flesh in a slow journey up the nail. It will be there for months to come, reminding me of my vulnerability, my slowing reflexes and aging self. I determine to be more mindful, more careful, more deliberate in my actions and less spontaneous. These animals can hurt me, as can their surroundings.

I expect September to be a quiet month at Lambsquarters. It is a time when our harvests are almost complete; the crops still ripening in the neighbouring fields are the purview of other farmers. Our hay and straw are set for winter, the second cut hay stacked separately to be saved for picky postnatal ewes. The garden produce is almost finished, only a few late beans that won't give up this year, carrots protected under straw, and pumpkins and squash waiting to grow sweeter with a touch of frost. I can leave the garden for a bit, leave the farm.

For many years, September was the beginning of my calendar year, a time I left the farm a few days a week. Once my children were well established in school, I returned to an academic life. It was a hectic time, combining farming with teaching. Looking back, I marvel at how I managed to fit it all in.

On days away, the barn chores came first, often before dawn, then a quick change from dungarees into professional clothes, and I was off to the university. Occasionally I had nightmares that I had forgotten my shoes and had to lecture in my wellies. It was a bit of a double life. Farmer to feminist scholar, shepherd to literature lecturer.

At the time, I felt a need for a more intellectual life. I had run dry living in isolation. Having colleagues and students opened my mind to new ideas and gave me confidence to write. And farming gave me a unique background; my first published paper was of pigs in a James Joyce story. Apparently no one had noticed the agricultural language before.

Eventually the low pay, the snowy roads, and the long hours overwhelmed me, and I gave it up. I began to write book reviews for a national newspaper and articles for magazines. I soon realized I could find intellectual stimulation right here on the farm. My sheep insinuated themselves into my writing.

Even twenty years later, every September feels like a new beginning. A time to pursue new experiences. I'm ready for a break after the pink eye, the flies, the humidity. I long to clear the perma-dirt from my fingernails, the grime and stain that nothing, even a lemon, can properly cleanse. How much longer will I be capable of travel? How much older will I get before it becomes too difficult, too cumbersome, too frightening?

I used to assume that aging would diminish any concern about taking risks. As I get closer to the end of my life, I should have less fear of things going amiss. After all, there are fewer years left. Why not give up caution, take more chances, travel to more remote, more dangerous places? What do I have to lose if the life left is so short?

Years ago, a weaver came to visit. She had picked up a hitch-hiker on her way, a man who disclosed having been in prison. I was shocked that she'd taken such a chance. Her response was that she was older and so the risk wasn't so great. She no longer had to support her family; her children were grown. She felt she could do whatever she wanted as the consequences were hers alone. She took more risks as she aged.

I think of her often and of how I expected to do the same. But like so many aging individuals, I seem to be more fearful as the years pile on. I do not want to live beyond meaningful capability; I resist decrepitude. Disability and morbidity worry me far more than mortality. I need to work harder to maintain my level of fitness, and I do not want to jeopardize my good health.

When I was young, I travelled through Europe by myself. I brashly hitchhiked alone, only taking the precaution of putting my thumb out in a spot before an intersection so I could suss out the vehicle before getting in, so I could ask where they were going. If I didn't like the look of them (or him), I said I was heading the other way. As if I could make competent judgments. I felt infallible, fully capable of managing the risks I was taking. Only once, travelling with a man alone, did I feel uncertain when he asked me if I was afraid. Not until then. I had wonderful encounters. An old couple in a beat-up banger, a young man who was picking up a baby carriage for his newborn, a pack of mountain climbers, a van full of stoned hippies, a couple with a screaming child who needed distraction, a transport driver who kept stopping for coffee and brandy and wanted someone to keep him awake. It could all have gone so wrong.

Becoming a parent made me careful. And even though my children are grown and gone, I have grandchildren who expect me to carry on. They think I'll live forever, think I'll enjoy being a hundred. And while I have no intention of living that long, I do feel a responsibility to stick around for a bit and be as capable and well as I can. And age brings this awful cumulative experience and knowledge of the world. Of the dangers and obstacles and diseases lying in wait. Watching too many friends suffer with artificial joints, with walkers and canes, having heart disease, diabetes, dementia. My mentors are all dead, some prematurely and some after long lives. The queue is getting shorter, and my place in it creeps ever closer to the front of the line. Decline is just as inevitable as death, but no easier to anticipate or accommodate.

A short vacation is in order. The plan is to stay in a lighthouse keeper's cottage in the Hebrides. The highlands and islands of Scotland are littered with sheep, so it will be a bit of a busman's holiday, but it offers the valuable concept of change. It will be a break from the worries of this farm and an opportunity to acquire new farming knowledge.

To prepare, I take my walking more seriously. Thomas joins me most days. The lighthouse has no road access. We will have to hike in and out carrying our supplies. We will need to be fit. I start to walk with a backpack, each day adding another book to get used to the weight I'll need to carry.

It's a scurry to get everything ready to leave the farm, even for only nine days. There are still infected eyes and daily treatments of washing, drops, and spray. I write in my farm book "spray and pray," desperate for their recovery. I know my barn nanny will cope with whatever happens, but I hate to leave her with extra tasks. Two ewes will stay inside until we get home, and she will treat them if necessary.

Late September is usually busy with trucking lambs to market, doing a last worming, a final pasture trim. But I'm pushing everything forward, working hard to pack in the tasks early. The hayfield must rest at this time to protect the alfalfa from winter kill, so there will be no pasturing there. I attach the rough-cut mower to the tractor and trim all the paddocks in the meadow and pie-shaped fields, except for the one closest to the barnyard where the sheep will graze until we get back.

Thomas splits firewood and begins to fill the woodshed while I cut the lawn, deadhead the flowers, dig up the calla lilies and rosemary, and pot them up for winter. Bemoan the possibility that frost will kill the nasturtiums and morning glories climbing up the side of the house before I return. I collect seeds from the California poppies, the calendula, and sweet peas, and I put in a late crop of greens: lettuce, arugula, and spinach, hopeful for a fall harvest in October. To prepare for Thanksgiving, I bring most of the pumpkins and squash into the barn for protection from a hard frost. I move the braided onions and garlic hanging from the rafters into the root cellar in the house, and I rather sadly fill the hummingbird feeder one last time, knowing they will have flown south before I return. I make lists and tick off the tasks, compress the month into its first few weeks.

The day comes, Kathryn is prepared to look after the farm, my list for her hanging on a nail in the feed room, and we leave for the airport. Winds are as high as 100 kilometres per hour. The unusually hot, humid air clashes with a cold front from the north, and there are six tornadoes in the eastern part of the province, houses smashed, trees down, wires broken. Ten thousand are without power. It feels unsettled here, and the winds are strong. We arrive at the airport in plenty of time, but our plane is late coming in. It has had to fight through massive headwinds to get here, and we will be seriously delayed. We are calm, no problem, there should still be time to catch our connecting flight in Dublin. Eventually we leave the ground and travel safely. However, it becomes quite clear as the hours pass that we will definitely miss our connection. This wouldn't be much of a problem, except that after the second flight, we must catch a train from Glasgow to Oban, board a ferry to Mull, get on a bus in Craignure, and get to Tobermory to buy food before the shops close. I've packed headlamps, but I dearly hope we won't have to make our final trek along a narrow cliff trail to find our remote lighthouse in the dark. And I have no idea, sitting on the plane, if there will be another flight, another train, another ferry, another bus.

How different from the days when I had no idea where my thumb would take me — where I would sleep that night or go the next day.

A combination of helpful flight attendants, access to the internet, international roaming telephone rates, and a well-functioning transportation system all coalesce to make new connections work. We are late arriving, but it is still daylight. The shops are open for our food, our wine, our beer. The fire is laid in the grate, and that first night, after more than twenty-four hours of travelling, it is clear without and cozy within.

The heritage Stevenson lighthouse gleams in the moonlight, its white column and ochre dome commanding the calm water around it, its beam projected at prescribed intervals out to the sea. In the morning, we look over to the far shore at Ardnamurchan, gleaming in sunshine. By the time we leave the cottage to hike into town, there is a magnificent double rainbow over the water, followed swiftly by a torrent of hail. We are far from home; we have no chores to do; we are well dressed for the weather and well fed on Scottish oats.

From the train, we'd seen many sheep in the rough hills of the west highlands. Scottish Blackface mostly, incredibly hardy double-coated horned sheep with speckled black faces and legs. We spied some Cheviots, which at home we pronounce like a French word, but here has a hard *ch* like the hills of the upland range to the east where they were named. They have a good carcass and make excellent crosses for meat production. I've used a Cheviot ram with my Border Leicesters in the past for market lambs. They are sturdy and growthy and handsome with pure white faces and legs, black noses and expressive ears. Their wool is short and springy, bulky and low lustre, so not as desirable for handspinning. Together with the Scottish Blackface, however, the Cheviot wool has a long history in the tweed industry, making a strong, weatherproof fabric that stands up to the wet winds of the west of the country. Harris Tweed famously uses wool from these breeds, the odd hairy kemp fibres showing white in the tweed where they do not take up dye.

Many years ago, we ferried to the isles of Lewis and Harris, where they make the tweed. We visited Roddy McKay, who wove, like so many others, on a Hattersley loom in his garden shed. It's a very different type of weaving from what I do. The looms are heavy iron, not wood, and mechanized to a degree. They work on foot pedals and a flying shuttle which throws the weft threads back and forth automatically. Roddy would sit with his hands on the front bar of the loom, his feet working swiftly, and the fabric would appear like magic in a pattern predetermined by the threading of the heddles.

He kept the leftover warp threads, called thrums, always attached to the loom, ready to be tied on to the next commission, as each parcel of tweed would be the same sett — the same number of threads per inch. Warps were dropped off at the side of the road by his cottage, already pre-wound at the mill, where the raw fleece was washed, dyed, carded, blended, and spun. When his length of tweed was finished, he folded it up and put it right out in the weather, back at the bottom of his lane, where the Harris Tweed factory vehicle would pick it up to go back to the mill for careful examination before it was washed, fulled, and finished for sale. There was always weather. The islands are almost bare of trees and open to the gales of the North Atlantic. Like the sheep themselves, the tweeds repel the rain.

We were lucky to meet his relative Kathy and spend an afternoon at her nearby house. She was spinning using part of an old wooden chair leg, turning it like a drop spindle to get the twist. I'm sure she could have found herself a spinning wheel, or a true drop spindle, but she was quite happy with what she had and her yarn was fine and even.

Sheep cover the islands, and I picked up wool from fences and scraped lichen from rocks to make the dye they call crotal. In the south of Harris, at Plocropol, we met Marion Campbell, who spun and dyed and wove tweed on a traditional wooden loom. On the day we visited her cottage, she was working on a beautiful piece of green tweed with hinted flecks of blue and yellow. She had nothing to sell that day but agreed to let me buy the tweed she was working on when it was finished later in the week. What joy it was to go back and find the finished fabric, fully washed, waulked, and ready for me. I've read that years later she became well-known for her work, and tourists flocked to her door hoping to meet her and buy her cloth. How fortunate I was to have been sent by Roddy McKay before she became famous.

When I attempted to visit the mill in Stornoway, I was refused admission. They didn't allow the public. But around back, when the workers were having their tea break, I got chatting wool with one of the men who took me in and gave me a tour. He showed me through the whole process from raw wool to finished tweed, and before I left through that back door, he gave me a couple of large spindles of spun wool, bits left over from warp- and weft-making. I brought it all home, wove my own fabric with the yarn, and made myself a jacket with Miss Campbell's tweed.

※.※

The wool industry is not lucrative these days. Even in Scotland and England, the historic heart of production, the prices are low for raw wool and interest has waned. Harris Tweed is seeing a revival of sorts but not particularly in the production of men's suits, jackets, and overcoats. Synthetic materials have replaced wool for outerwear. They are much lighter and repel rather than absorb the rain. Fabric made from plastic bottles is fashioned into an unnatural fuzzy cloth erroneously called fleece, which is about as far from a sheep's fleece as possible. It pollutes our waterways and oceans by shedding quantities of microplastic and melts to the skin if burned. Wool resists flame.

The Harris Tweed symbol is less prevalent these days. In Mull, we found it only on small items, coin purses, handbags, and spectacle cases. There are weavers still on the Outer Hebrides, and the brand is protected by an act of Parliament. The tweed must be "handwoven by the islanders at their homes in the Outer Hebrides, finished in the Outer Hebrides, and made from pure virgin wool dyed and spun in the Outer Hebrides." The virgin wool designation indicates the wool is directly from the sheep and not recycled. It has nothing to do with the age, gender, or breeding history of the sheep. Harris Tweed is made in various weights now, looking for new markets in hard-wearing upholstery, superfine fashion, and featherweight accessories, even adorning shoes.

Mull, an inner Hebridean island, is close to the mainland, and its east side is treed. The path to the lighthouse winds through a thick canopy, steep sides, rocky outcrops, and dashing waterfalls, cascades and cataracts. The wet climate assures continuous streams rush down in chutes from the top of the hills, and footing is tenuous, even treacherous on narrow spots when it's wet. When the sun shines, as it does periodically most days, the light dapples through the leaves and the plethora of vines that grow up nearly every tree trunk of the stunted hazel and oak woodlands collectively known as Celtic Rainforest. Shades of green seem endless and ever-changing in the constantly variable light.

Above the seaside bank lie the flat pastures and treeless hills where the sheep graze. The Blackface and Cheviots are hill sheep quite capable of venturing up into the mist on narrow verdant tracks without faltering. They live outside all year, often lamb on the hillsides, and spend only the harshest times in yards or pastures near their farmsteads. A flock of grazing piebald Jacob sheep displays spotted fleeces and decorative long horns near the main road.

Part of the reason for choosing to visit Mull is a course offered by the Scottish Farm Advisory Service on resilience planning for sheep. It is one of a number of meetings held across Scotland, an on-farm event encouraging farmers to learn better ways to optimize their flock health and to get the best returns for their product. They kindly invited us to attend and make us feel most welcome. The farm is a distance from the lighthouse, with no public transportation. We do not have telephone coverage, but it being the twenty-first century, there is Wi-Fi and we are able to email a taxi company and arrange to be met at a designated spot in town near our trailhead.

When the driver picks us up, he seems puzzled. Because of my surname, he and his partner have tried to figure out just exactly who I am. Mull is the historic seat of the clan MacLean, so they assume I must be local, my email giving no hint of my provenance. The name is spelled variously MacLean, Maclean, McLean.

A history scholar informed me that spelling was initially completely arbitrary, and that documents as recently as the nineteenth century frequently use different spellings of the name on the same page. Some of my distant relatives favour Mac, but as far as I can follow my direct family line, we've never used the first *a*. Our cabbie is quite amused to discover that we're Canadian and going to a sheep conference at that. We are neither local nor the sort of tourist he is used to.

Mull has the atmosphere of a close-knit community. We assume we will probably need a taxi back when the day is over, but consider the possibility that someone will be going our way. Farmers are generous; someone is likely to offer us a ride. Our taxi driver says he can't pick us up at the required time as he has to fetch his children from school, so he'd have to come early. We leave it that we will telephone if we need him.

The course at first is less formal than I expected. Indeed there are expert presenters: a sheep specialist, a veterinary investigating officer, and a farm manager from Scotland's Rural College Hill and Mountain Research Farms. There are about fifty people attending, all dressed warmly in suitable barn attire, which is just as well as our meeting is held in a dilapidated open stone shed. Benches are set up and there's a screen at the front for the PowerPoint presentations, but the floor is covered in straw, mud, dags, and second cuts from countless shearings. Everything is open to the weather on one side, and heavy equipment and bales of wool have been pushed along one wall to make room for us and for the tables where tea breaks and lunch are being organized.

Ewan opens the meeting with a gracious greeting, happy with the effort people have made to be here. There are farmers from every part of Mull, from the mainland, and there's even an international contingent from as far away as Canada, he says, looking at us, and jokes that perhaps we are here to broker a trade deal because of Brexit. He mentions that we would appreciate a ride back to Tobermory if anyone is going our way, then introduces Poppy, the sheep specialist and our first speaker. Enthusiastic, strawberry-blonde ponytail swinging, she takes us through the importance of flock health and management both pre- and post-tupping.

Because lambs are vulnerable high on the surrounding hills, these farmers are hoping their ewes will conceive and raise just one lamb per season. Twins and triplets are likely to be smaller, weaker, and more likely to get separated from their dams in the wide spaces of their pastures, so the farmers try to manage nutrition to have ewes somewhat lean before putting in the rams. On our farm, where we attend lambing in the barn, we always hope for twins and usually manage 150 percent or higher with the Border Leicesters. We want our ewes to go into breeding in good condition, with a palpable amount of muscle and body fat. Too thin and they might not be able to raise twins; too fat and they might not conceive.

Poppy divides us into two groups. Our group follows her across the mucky yard into another stone shed while the others stay behind to hear from the vet about liver flukes. A group of Blackface sheep is penned in a chute, each wearing a cardboard tag with a number. Before we approach them, Poppy illustrates body score conditioning on an easel pad set up in the barn. She goes through the concept of the testing and writes down the various levels with a rating from one to five. It's critical, she tells us, to know the condition of our ewes long enough before breeding to be able to get them in proper shape. It will take six weeks on better feed to bring them up a point on the chart.

She demonstrates and then hands around pieces of sheep bone that have been encased in shearling hide. The bones are the lower part of the spine, include five or six vertebrae with its ridges, called the spinous process, and the attached short ribs or transverse process. Like the animals, they also are numbered from one to five, and the space between the woolly covering and the bones varies much as it does on live sheep of comparable condition. The props provide a clever way for us to practise — to feel exactly what we should expect on each level of animal so we can check our own flocks at home.

Poppy sets up a new sheet on her easel with boxes to tick for each animal. We are to go through and check the sheep — she's calling them gimmers — and then mark the condition score we've determined on the chart. The farmers are uniformly quiet, hanging back a bit, reluctant to begin. I gather this is new territory for some of them, though it is something we are familiar with and have been practising on our sheep for a number of years. Poppy seems surprised that we know the system.

Someone manages to go first and the rest of us follow — like sheep. The animals are well chosen: one is gaunt, a definite one; another is very fat, a five. Others hover around the midpoint, but it is not too difficult to decipher a difference. If I can feel no muscle or fat over the ridge of the spine, can get my fingers right into the spaces between the short ribs, this animal is likely not going to make it to breeding weight in time. She's a one. A bit of muscle makes another seem like a two; I can still feel her spine and the edges of the short ribs, though they are not sharp like the first. The five is so fat that I can't feel any bones at all. With the four, I can just make out the spinous process, and the three has an adequate covering, but I perceive the bones beneath. After I'm finished, I go up to a kind-looking young woman and ask her what a gimmer is. I can tell these are young ewes — likely lambs born last spring — but I'm unfamiliar with the term. She tells me it's a ewe lamb kept for breeding, but before she's had her first lamb. A Scottish term.

There's a bit of milling about, quite a lot of disparity marked on the chart, and clearly some confusion. But everyone has a handout to refer to, and perhaps we'll all be a bit better at this now. Certainly Thomas and I were impressed with the woolly spines we'd practised with, and we determine to check our flock again when we return home.

Time for a break with homemade biscuits and cakes, steaming mugs of coffee or tea. Cauldrons bubbling on the background burners bode well for lunch. The groups switch, and we go back to our seats on the benches for a lecture on liver flukes by Heather, a veterinarian.

The fluke is a parasite that develops in the bile ducts of sheep causing anaemia, weight loss, dullness, and even death. Their eggs pass through the sheep into fresh water, hence their prevalence on this wet terrain. When they hatch, they infect minute snails about the size of the graphite on the tip of a pencil. After a number of weeks, they are shed in the water and vegetation, and when the sheep graze the area, they ingest the larvae that eventually mature to adult flukes, which then set up housekeeping in the liver.

Heather has a sophisticated PowerPoint presentation, somewhat incongruous in this rough setting and at the same time absolutely appropriate. There's a pen of rams behind and below the projection screen, visible from a barred opening if you look down, and periodically they offer comment. My mind wanders somewhat; apparently we do have liver flukes in Canada, but I've never been aware of them. Our pastures are dry most of the summer and inaccessible in winter, so we are not bothered by wet areas. Lambsquarters does have a natural wetland, but the only time we graze anywhere near it is when it too has dried up in an arid summer, and we need the extra grass at its edge.

I stop daydreaming when Heather plays a video of a sheep post-mortem. Out of the depths of a dead animal, a liver is shown moving, seething, disgorging live flukes. They are green, slimy, disgusting, and the liver itself is covered in lesions. The damage they do can cause all manner of problems beyond the liver from abortion to metabolic disease, to infections and general weakness and stress.

The next part of her programme educates the farmers on what anti-fluke wormers to use on their flocks and when. It is critical to treat the right stage of fluke at the right time. Heather advises restricting access to wet areas, fencing off streams, but there's no such thing as a dry pasture in all of Scotland, I don't imagine, and certainly not in the Hebrides. It is crucial for these farmers to understand the products available to help them keep liver flukes under control. We gather around as Heather throws a pile of empty worming medication containers onto the floor. We are asked to take one, read the instructions, and then call out the proper product when she presents the theoretical circumstance.

It is a tricky business. Different products work on different stages of the fluke life cycle at different times of the year and with differing problems of drug resistance. These farmers have to work hard to figure out what to use when. With climate change, Heather tells us, wet summers are predicted to get even worse over the next twenty years, and overuse and incorrect dosage are likely to increase drug resistance. She encourages management strategies to reduce risks — shipping lambs early before they are infected, quarantining afflicted animals until they respond to treatment, monitoring anaemia by checking for pale eyelids on individual sheep, fencing off snail habitats, removing flocks from the wettest pastures, improving drainage, planting brassicas for grazing, and housing lambs to finish for market.

She finishes up, gathers her empty anthelmintic containers, and we are invited to have our lunch. Farmers are a hardy bunch. It's cold, wet, and we've worked hard to take all this in, so in spite of the recent disgusting video, we all find ourselves queueing up politely to receive a comforting bowl of soup and a barbecued burger. Cakes, squares, and chocolate appear for dessert, and the urns provide fresh coffee and tea. We mingle a bit, but these are taciturn Scots and, apart from the organizers, we make little headway. We may be farmers, but we are also clearly tourists — the only ones.

No rides have been offered, but I wait until the afternoon break to call the taxi to pick us up. When that time comes, after more presentations and lots of discussion of markets for hill lambs, we discover there is no mobile or internet coverage. Neither our phones nor anyone else's can get a signal. What about the farmhouse? I ask. Well, there's no one there at the moment, and the farm manager is here making a presentation. Absentee landlord? I never discover, but I'm starting to get anxious. It took us a good half hour to get here by car — clearly too far to walk at the end of the day — and there's no bus. Too late I realize that Tobermory is at the end of the road. No one will be passing through. I feel like an idiot and a nuisance when one of the organizers says they won't see us short. They will inconvenience themselves to get us back, but it seems they are leaving the island and must catch the ferry back to the mainland.

And then I see a benevolent-looking couple conferring. They turn and tell us they will take us back. I demur, worried about them going out of their way, but no, the woman says, she needs to pick up something from the vet in Tobermory. It's a trip she needs to make. They are Enid and Geoffrey, retired from the mainland to Mull to raise Hebridean sheep, an ancient and local breed — small, short-tailed, with black or dark brown wool. Like the other hill sheep, they have horns, often four. Geoffrey confirms that wool prices are terrible here — nine pence a pound at the co-op — but he and Enid are able to sell their wool to a local mill for a much better price.

We are so thankful to be given a ride and happy to bounce around on rough roads in the back seat engulfed in the smell of wet dog. Even more thankful when we discover that the vet is not actually in Tobermory, but some miles without. The kindness of strangers.

It's been an instructive day, but cold and wet, and before striking out on our trail to the lighthouse, we find the pub at a local hotel, settle in front of an open fire, and warm ourselves with a wee spot of alcohol.

From the buildings on the beautiful high street, each painted a different bright hue, we can see that Tobermory is a tourist spot in season. There are restaurants, hotels, a distillery, and lots of gift shops. The bookstore is spectacular, filled with local history, ornithology, geography; an outfitting shop suggests that this is a jumping-off place for adventurers. There are nature tours, fishing jaunts, excursions to the outer islands, particularly Iona and Staffa. There is also a ferry to the mainland, which we take on a sunny day to Ardnamurchan. We stay long enough to have lunch and walk around the area where once only crofters lived. Their cottages have been made into holiday lets now, the old hard way of life gone for good.

I do find a spinner though, and we compare notes. There is wool for sale from the local mill, including tiny balls wound and presented in a half-dozen egg carton, each a different natural shade from white through grey to black. The high price is aimed at the tourist, not the knitter, and they surely can't sell enough to work through the thousands of fleeces shorn here each year. There are more sheep in Scotland than people.

A weaver is selling her wares at the local market. She makes cushion covers and broaches from ends of yarn she buys from the mill in Lewis. She can't call her fabric Harris Tweed, as it is not woven in the Outer Hebrides, but she faithfully follows the traditional designs, adding original colourways. The crofts are gone, but the crafts continue.

※ ※

On our last day, we take a boat to Staffa. It's a fair drive across the island in a minibus to get to the jetty and then a chilly trip in a boat big enough for twenty passengers. We are dressed warmly and have packed a lunch, including a small bottle of wine. There are many small islands off the west coast, many seals basking on the shore. The seal pups are just maturing, though some of them still show white. They are unfazed by our presence, nonchalant.

When we come to the edge of Staffa, we are overwhelmed by the hexagonal basalt columns littering the shoreline. They are so precise, so carefully carved that it's difficult to believe they are made by nature. As the boat swings into the entrance of Fingal's Cave, the sun is brilliant, lighting up the interior and dazzling the dark blue waters. Mendelssohn plays in my mind.

We hike to the south side of the uninhabited island, spread out our picnic, and lie in the sun. It seems the other passengers are exploring the cave, not something I'm inclined to do, so we have the moor to ourselves. Wildflowers abound, seabirds circle, the view is sublime.

On the way back to town, in a private car driven by the captain's daughter, we pass flocks of grazing sheep. Suddenly I spot a cast ewe. Her legs are flailing: she can't get over. I call out, but the driver either does not hear or chooses not to. How I want to yell at her to stop the car — to let me out so I can hop the fence and help the ewe to her feet. But I do not. There are other passengers. I am a stranger in this land. Perhaps it is not my place. I can only hope the animal survived.

October

Before leaving Scotland, we spend an afternoon in the local Tobermory museum. Along with the usual military uniforms and historical dioramas, there is a disturbing section on the island clearances.

Until a few years ago, I'd always assumed that my McLean ancestors had been cleared from their land to make way for sheep. Over 150,000 Scots were forced from their homes and immigrated to the Americas and the Antipodes between the 1780s and the 1880s. My family left Inverness-shire in 1831 and 1833. Donald, in his twenties, went ahead with other young neighbours and made arrangements for his parents and ten siblings to join him later. I've always known where they settled in Canada, down country from where I now farm. But when my cousin put me in touch with David Taylor, the Scottish historian, I discovered my family's specific history and visited the homestead. I learned they were tenant farmers who made money to pay rent, not crofters who earned their small landholdings by providing labour to landowners. My forebears made a living by raising cattle and thereby had agency over their future. Their lives were rough and difficult, living in a dark thatched cottage with a dirt floor, the animals at one end, the family at the other, an open chimney-less fire in the centre. They practised transhumance, moving with the animals in the summer from their home glen up into the hills to small stone huts called shielings. The hardy black cattle thrived on common land in the highlands through the warmer months, then some were sold before winter. Drovers herded them south on foot as far as the lucrative Smithfield market in London, where tens of thousands were traded each year.

The McLeans grew a small amount of grain on their poor valley land, kale and other vegetables, but without rich grasses to make much hay, they were limited as to how many animals they could shelter in winter. They would have had a few sheep for their own use — to spin and weave and knit. They bred the cows, kept the calves, and sold off the steers and extra heifers. The money they made not only covered their rent but allowed them to accumulate enough to leave Scotland.

The McLeans, with six other families, were not evicted but chose to leave in a planned migration. They had the money to buy their passage and were not driven destitute to the coast to forage for themselves, or to the coffin ships like so many others. Their land, unlike much of the highlands and islands, was not given over to sheep; it was let to the Duke and Duchess of Bedford, who began to restrict highland grazing in favour of sporting. The duchess, Georgiana, "turned the upper glen into a playground for her rich friends." After years of bad weather, failed harvests, and floods, the future must have looked grim. It was time to leave, and Canada called.

I was shocked to discover their primitive Scottish lifestyle, particularly as I saw how prosperous they quickly became. One generation produced a brick house bigger than my own and educated a teacher, a physician, and a lawyer. When they arrived, the land was covered in virgin pine forest. At first, they cut logs to build a basic house; by the autumn, they had cleared enough land to seed a crop of winter wheat. They were familiar with hardship, with the wild weather of the Cairngorms, with work. But here were new methods of farming, so much more land. Though the winters were harsh, the summers were warm and so favourable to cultivation. When I look back to the early years on my farm, coping with primitive facilities, I am ashamed to remember the relatively minor discomforts. My forbears were so tough, so brave.

Mull is the seat of the McLean clan, and I discover that some McLeans, if not subjected to the clearances, were implicated. The small museum in Tobermory has handwritten documents of landowners who evicted their crofters and tenants. And one of them has my surname.

I find my family culpable. From exploitation of First Nations by my maternal many-greats-grandfather Thomas Gummersall Anderson, who was an Indian agent in Upper Canada before Confederation, to my paternal McLean clan involved in Scottish eviction. Though my immigrant ancestors were not evicted, the land they were sold in the New World was not uninhabited. Situated some 100 kilometres south of where I farm, they settled on the site of an Indigenous village; the tracts bought from the Crown had been inhabited around 1500 CE by the semi-nomadic

Attawandaron, or Neutral, Nation, who typically settled in one place for about twenty years in longhouses, hunting, fishing, and cultivating the fertile soil. Long before my ancestors arrived, the Attawandaron were all but annihilated by conflicts and by diseases, like measles and smallpox, brought by earlier settlers. Their nation collapsed, and those who survived dispersed into other communities. Historic burial grounds continued to surface, artifacts revealed by my relatives' ploughs, until an archaeological dig in the 1980s revealed the remains of a five-hectare village of four thousand inhabitants.

From the late seventeenth century, the Mississaugas of the Credit First Nation seasonally occupied the territory. Just as the Scots practised transhumance to graze their herds in the summer, Indigenous families left their southern settlements to hunt in winter. By the time the McLeans arrived, the land had shamefully been acquired by the colonial government, and the Mississaugas were forced farther afield by the influx of Euro-Canadian settlement.

I expect my ancestors were unaware their migration followed the forced removal of First Nations from the land they acquired. Until they found arrowheads and graves, they might not have known the fields were once inhabited. I doubt they thought of themselves as an invasive force. Unlike too many current global migrants, the government here welcomed them, fully encouraged them to come. The colonial establishment sought to recreate and augment itself with fellow Europeans. First Nations were expected to assimilate to the mores of the immigrants, and they continue to experience trauma from generations of imposition, displacement, and abuse.

Political turmoil and war have created untenable conditions for many migrants today, and the climate crisis will substantially swell their numbers. Frequently they are not welcomed, even by people who migrated themselves. Although Canada has been relatively supportive of refugees recently, the former prime minister, Stephen Harper, directed his unsuccessful final re-election campaign at what he called "old stock" Canadians, favouring families with roots in Europe. There is a frightening undercurrent of fear of and resentment against immigration by those who choose to ignore that absolutely all but Indigenous Peoples in this country are immigrants themselves.

My own place on this continuum is problematic. Of course, I too am an immigrant; some of my ancestors left Europe as long ago as the 1600s, the most recent in the early 1900s. When the time comes to cede my farm, will I pass it on to my descendants in the same vein? Or should I return it to First Nations or give it to recent refugees? It is a question I must consider. For now, I try my best to steward that land, to leave a legacy of care that honours its original inhabitants.

花.求

My Scottish immigrant family must have suffered in their first Canadian winters, but they would have understood inclement weather. For our journey to Scotland, we were prepared for squalls and gusts, but we did not expect to come home to incessant grey skies and rain in the Canadian autumn. October on the farm should be a month of brilliant colour in the woods, backlit by dazzling sun. Where everything on Mull was green, all is dull red and gold here, sadly muted in the persistent cloud cover. Because of the weather, not much has changed on the farm while we were away. It's been too wet for our neighbours to harvest the beans, combine the corn.

Thanksgiving seems early this year, with less time for me to prepare after being away. My son flies home from the west with his dog, my daughter and her family arrive with their new puppy, and the house is full, messy, alive. Not big enough for everyone. A few years ago, we realized we needed a new sleeping space, a bunky. Back behind the barn, we built the Lamba, named for a piece of cloth from Madagascar that had a hand in its construction. It is a square cabin, made of wood with windows on all sides, cedar shingles on its peaked roof, hardwood on the floor. It serves as a writing shed, a retreat from farm work at the end of a long summer day, but its prime function is to shelter my son when he visits from the west. He's a tall man. He needs space, his own space.

Always I have treasured Thanksgiving as the best holiday. There are no presents, no disappointments. There is reasonable, and often fabulous, weather, and the days are only just beginning to shorten, keeping seasonal affective disorder at bay. Our tradition is to serve only food that is grown at Lambsquarters. Instead of turkey, that American pilgrim pleasure, we roast a leg of lamb or two, Thomas carving at one end of the table and our son at the other. Father and son face off with knives in a peaceful and nurturing duel. As they carve, my daughter and I dish out quantities of floury potatoes, squash roasted with maple syrup, green beans laced with garlic. The dogs, Cinder and Parka, lie under the table, hoping for scraps to drop, and grandsons Ian and Alistair often accidentally oblige with their raucous table manners. For dessert, there are pies. Pumpkin, raspberry, apple. I do not grow my own wheat for the pastry, though one year I did make cookies from grain I gleaned from the field across the way.

My centrepiece is a harvest bread shaped in a sheaf of wheat, tied with a braid of crisp dough and topped with a small decorative edible mouse. It is tricky to make, to judge the shapes before the dough rises, but this year it turns out well, the mouse quite lifelike with its peppercorn eyes and curling tail.

The boys get out the hockey net, sticks, and balls, and the dogs join in and make a nuisance of themselves. There are long walks and intimate talks, competitive croquet on the lawn, beer and wine on the verandah stretching the day into night, punctuated by frequent honking from flocks of geese flying south over the farm. It's a short holiday with no commercial lead-up, no expectations, so everyone is cordial, comfortable, calm.

While they are here, my family gets to work. They bring in more firewood, put up storm windows, sweep the chimney. Their youth and strength help us prepare for winter. And once again, I realize my age. I no longer stack wood. I no longer climb ladders. And preparing the food takes more energy and planning than ever before. I question whether I continue to do this Thanksgiving celebration dinner because everyone expects me to, or because they are perhaps afraid to interfere. So far I seem to manage, and I feel my family's respect for my autonomy, their recognition of my stubborn adherence to the tradition I've set. I determine to keep on. As long as there are sheep in the field and vegetables in the garden. It is an incentive to keep shepherding to feed my family from the farm they grew up on. It is a harvest festival and depends on my tenacity to shepherd, to sow, and to reap.

※.※

Frost is late this year. Where once we could expect it by Labour Day, just as the kids were going back to school, with climate change the autumns are warmer and warmer. The gardens continue to produce. Beans grow well beyond their expected harvest, and carrots are still there to be dug fresh. The house is decorated with gourds that volunteered all over the garden in the spring; their seeds must have survived in the compost. When I found them germinating, I carefully transplanted many of them to one corner and let them vine their way around and behind the wooden bench I rarely find time to rest on. At first, I thought they were squash, butternut from a meal I'd made in early spring, their seeds perhaps sifting to the bottom of the compost pile that had been spread early on. As they grew, however, it was clear they were decorative. Striped, knobby, shades of darkest green to brightest orange and yellow. They have long thin necks or star-shaped bodies, and I fill a whole bushel basket with them to top a stone wall outside and grace a cornucopia within.

Zinnias flash brilliant colours, their reds and pinks vie for recognition over the vibrant nasturtiums still climbing, and the heavenly blue morning glories spill over the old gate given from Maik's former garden next door. In the borders by the house, monkshood shimmer their blue-violet bonnets; snakeroot flowers scent the air with jasmine; windflowers sway in prevailing breezes. Native blossoms dot the plateau: fall asters, goldenrod, coneflower. But not for long. Soon the wet weather turns cold, and frost dusts the morning ground. Nasturtiums wilt, zinnias shrivel and brown, and morning glory vines sag on their strings. Everything must be cut down. Leaves fall, litter the yard, sully the gardens.

It is finally dry enough to harvest the soybean crop. Then just after my neighbours finish combining, they manoeuvre the massive air seeder onto the field. They no longer plough, disc, harrow, seed, and roll in separate time-consuming and diesel-guzzling manner but plant their winter-wheat crop in one operation with a no-till implement. Coming down the road attached to the tractor, it looks like a huge alien, its large disc wings folded up, the massive yellow seed and fertilizer bins following behind, their hoses angling out like daddy-long-legs. In the field, the discs are lowered, the depth is set, and off it goes in one pass, slicing a trench, planting the seed, fertilizing, and covering it with earth. A series of rollers, also levered up for the road, follow to smooth the ground. The field is seeded right into the stubble of the previous bean crop that lies flat and tidy after the planting.

It's such a huge change from our first years here when farmers were ploughing, turning up rough clods of earth in furrows that then needed breaking up with discs and harrows. When finally the earth was friable enough to plant, the seed drill, an ancient contraption with wooden bins hand-filled with seed, was pulled over the field. More than once, I rode on Maik and Gerrit's, standing on a platform clinging desperately to the bins, checking to see they were still full, finding myself blackened with dust by the end of the day. After seeding down, the field was rolled in a separate operation, the roller consisting of an axle packed tight with a row of old rubber tires. It bore no resemblance to the shiny steel rollers following the John Deere we see now.

In the woods, leaves carpet the forest floor, still showing colour, the patterns impressionistic, like a pointillist painting. Until one day it snows heavily. Bitter north winds blow sideways across the fields, dusting the conifers, browning the fallen leaves. My winter barn coat, my toque, my mitts are made ready. I put away the summer clothes and go through the bin of hats and gloves. It's time to prepare for winter.

I get one more look at the baby foxes on the hill. On a sunny morning, they roll around like puppies, though they are now full-grown. They play bite-throat, one aggressive, one submissive, and I remember my first sightings of them months ago — the one who would come out of the den and watch me while the other stayed close, with a good self-protective instinct. They repeatedly dance away, then rush toward each other in their game before finally ducking through the wire fence and off into the bush. I'd seen their tracks days before in a skiff of snow. Will they show themselves again in winter? I'm sorry to think I might not be safely able to put my chickens outside next spring, but I cannot dislike these beautiful animals, so sleek in their demeanour, so stunning in their glossy red coats and black legs, their foxy faces and playful personalities. I wish them a good winter with plenty of mice to fill their bellies. The more they catch, the fewer will come into the house, overtake the barn.

Some years, I still have lambs to send to market in October, but because of the pink eye problem, they were all sold early this year. Except the replacement ewe lambs — who I now call gimmers after my education on Mull. To register them, we tattoo the inside of their ears. Our flock letters on the left, their number and the year letter on the right.

Tattooing is a quick process, and over the years, I've learned to make it easier and more effective. I spray a little cleanser on the ear, then wipe off the dirt and grease. The ink comes in a roll-on bottle similar to deodorant, and I give the ear a good swipe of green. Next the tattoo pliers make the tiny holes, another swipe of ink, and on to the next ear. A few moments and they are finished. Off they go, looking a little silly with the smear of green ink, but it disappears quickly and only the tattoo numbers and letters remain.

We use tags as well — baby brass tags at birth, and small plastic tags (white for ewe lambs, blue for rams). These small tags don't last very well, but they are lighter than the adult tags and don't drag the ears down. The replacement ewes get a bigger, stronger tag when they lamb. I carefully apply it in the same hole, rather like changing an earring in a pierced ear. It takes a pair of pliers to apply, but there is no pain. Not that they are particularly happy about being bothered.

To leave the farm, even to go to the vet or a show, all animals must have an RFID: radio-frequency identification tag. This way, any disease outbreaks or food safety issues are meant to be more easily traced. We are compelled to keep good records in order to identify any animal that might become problematic. In large flocks, all the sheep will be tagged this way, and farmers can keep track of weights and other information with tag readers and computer analysis. At Lambsquarters, we use them only when they leave the farm.

Recently I've noticed I can no longer read the tags from across the paddock or even across the pen. In the past, my eyesight was excellent; age seems to affect every sense.

The black ewes tend to have individual variation in fleece colour which I recognize, but the white ewes are fairly uniform; they can be difficult to distinguish. Feeding time is the best to identify an animal as I can get close when it's absorbed in its dinner.

With early snows and frosty mornings, the grass is offering less and less nutrition to the flock. Before the month is over, I bring them into the barnyard and begin feeding hay. They are always so delighted to get out to pasture in the spring, getting pickier and pickier about the hay when they can smell fresh grass growing, but conversely they seem just as excited to get at the dry fodder when they've been out all summer.

Before I feed out the first bale, we put blankets on the black sheep. These are show coats, heavy canvas coverings that go over their ears and come down their sides with straps to hook around their hind legs. It can be quite comical to get them on, like playing peek with a child's pullover, but once dressed, they seem happy and their fleeces are now perfectly protected from debris. I am careful with the feeders and the constituents of the hay, but any stems at all will ruin a valuable black fleece. In white wool, the tiny bits blend in, but in coloured wool, they visually dominate, and it's almost impossible to clean them out by hand. Commercial wool is carbonized with acid and heat to eliminate vegetable matter, but my fleeces all go to handspinners, who are very particular about visible chaff. The canvas dust covers help to keep the dark fleeces pristine.

In October, the wood stove comes back to life. When Thomas is busy with maple syrup in the spring, he gathers firewood. He has a system for cleaning up the forest floor and felling vintage dead and dying trees between his trips to feed the fire and empty sap buckets. I don't see much of him then; he leaves early in the morning and frequently stays all day even if I don't bring down lunch. As spring approaches and the snow melts, he gathers rotting deadfall and piles it to dry for the next syrup season, harvests trees that have failed over the winter, cuts up blowdowns.

Cedars uproot in high winds, and though he has successfully pulled some back and tethered them upright, many are beyond saving. These become fast fuel for making maple syrup, which we give away to family and friends and enjoy at home all year, and they are also excellent kindling. On a chopping block, he hatchets cedar chunks into thin sticks that catch a flame in a trice in the back-kitchen stove. Each October, they come into use.

When I was small and spent summers at my grandparents' cottage, I was surrounded by wood. In the forest and in the various woodsheds. My grandfather had a hired man, Harvey Carter, whom I now recognize as a kind of genius. He looked like Jimmy Durante, not very tall, wiry, big nose. He worked all day every day through the week, drove to the cottage in his Nash Rambler from his rooming house in town.

He kept all the woodsheds full, including the former ice house. They were divided by use, in my memory. Kindling, stove wood, hardwood. My grandmother cooked on an enamel wood stove, and they heated the cottage with a stone fireplace in the living room. Every morning, the stove was fired up for breakfast. The mornings were always cool in the cottage, which is set on a hill on a peninsula. I have memories of her perking coffee and cooking steak and eggs for my portly grandfather, though she was as thin as a sapling.

I was sometimes sent for fuel when I was small, just light kindling and stove lengths from the closest shed — the one by the flagstone path lined with a crazy quilt of tuberous begonias. I would carry a few loads and put them in the woodbox under my grandmother's fringed buckskin jacket hanging from the moose antlers above. Harvey delivered the big logs in a wheelbarrow, piled higher than he was, from the sheds down the hill.

Not only did he cut and split the wood, fill the sheds, fill the boxes, and sort the product according to use, he also looked after the entire property, which stretched over hundreds of forested acres. He hand-cut paths with a machete through the woods, cut lawns to precision, kept the buildings painted and sound, planted and tended gardens of roses, gladioli, and vegetables. He planted extensive drifts of daffodils — yellow, white, mixed. Wooden lawn chairs were painted and wheeled or boated to remote shorelines every spring, set up on rocks to alert visitors that this was not Crown land, though all anyone cared about was that picnickers did not light fires. Then Harvey gathered them up again in October and stored them in one of the boathouses over winter.

He created a water lily garden from a swamp and built a causeway to the small island beyond it with a central arched bridge; the design could have influenced Monet. Each day, he marked the number and colour of the lily blooms on the boathouse wall. When he wasn't gathering wood or tending gardens, or wading in the water to secure a raft or rebuild a dock crib, he was shooting groundhogs who got into his gardens, fixing motors on the boats. One time, he took a handsaw and cut the garage in half, pulled it apart, and built a new section in the middle to extend its length for my grandfather's new car. Basically he could do anything.

I would hang around Harvey if I could, but usually he was too busy for me to keep up, and I realize now he liked to work alone. There was a story, of course. I learned later that he had been a druggist, had been in the forces with my grandfather in the first war, had been unlucky in love, had some sort of breakdown, and began to work for my family. He was there all spring, summer, and fall, spending winters with his sister down country. I can only hope my grandfather treated him well; he could be a cruel man. But Harvey was loyal beyond explanation. When he retired, after my grandfather died, no one could take his place. The grounds fell to ruin.

With this knowledge of how wood could miraculously appear, perfectly cut, perfectly dried, perfectly suited for every aspect of fire-making, I came to Lambsquarters with unrealistic expectations. We bought the farm in October and visited on weekends before finally moving here in January. The kitchen had a wood-burning cookstove with pipes snaking through the ceiling into a buttressed chimney in one bedroom, through a hole in another for the pipe to heat the upstairs. Wood was essential until we installed a furnace, and the stove was valuable with its reservoir to heat water. There was a single cold water tap for the whole house.

We had a dilapidated woodshed with just enough wood to get us started and enough cold weather to teach us the importance of good fuel. The first few years, we bought a load of wood each October. It was delivered all in a pile in the lane. I had to learn how to stack it properly, to make reticulated corners, to tell the difference between a cord and a face cord. There were no wimpy face cords at the cottage, only full cords four feet by four feet by eight.

I expected proper kindling, small split hardwood, and stove-length logs. A tall order, and no Harvey Carter to fill it. Thomas, however, has the skills. For years, he used a maul for splitting; now he has a mechanical splitter that runs off the hydraulics on the tractor. He leaves the wood he gathered in the spring to dry for another year, stacks the previous year's harvest in the woodshed with a separate area for cedar kindling, a box for small hardwood, and rows and rows of dry logs. Harvey is with me still.

❦⟡

Before the weather turns impossible, Thomas rushes each morning to work on his wall. I pull out the remaining vines, the weeds, the plant debris, and the errant gourds to give him space. Because he's walling himself in, he must wheel his barrow through the garden gate to reach the last side, so I make a path for him between my bench and the last rows of greens. In the final days of the month, he finishes the base of the last corner, the heavy foundation stones laid, the batter wide and strong, the line true. It's slow work, a puzzle, a cryptic assembly combining geology, geometry, and genius. He refuses to quit in the rain, will not wear gloves in the cold as he needs to feel each rock. Needs to weigh it and turn it, determine its substance and deduce its place. When finally he stops for the day, dirt smears his face, cakes his knees, tattoos his hands. Shards of granite line his pockets where chips have flown from his stone hammer, his chisels. It won't be long before the weather forces him to gather his tools and store them away for the season. Reluctantly, he leaves the unfinished wall to sit silent and await the snow.

November

November is a time of reflection. After long days outside, in the flurry of autumn activity to prepare for winter, the bedding down of sheep in-bye, it is time to turn inward. As I age, time extends behind me in the ever-widening perspective of a country lane; ahead is the vanishing point. My position grows closer, perceptibly faster, to where the two lines meet. Uncertain, unpredictable, but inevitable. November is a time to consider, to ponder, to draw in.

As the weather worsens, I reluctantly gear up in jacket and wellies to feed the sheep, my hens, and Greenwood. As the days grow shorter and darker, I especially miss Flora's presence beside me, in the barn and back inside on her mat behind the fire.

The gardens are abandoned: perennials cut down, tender plants mulched. A bale of straw angles against the house to protect kitchen pipes from freezing. Every few days, I feed the birds, the species diminishing as the days grow short. Just woodpeckers and chickadees remain, and goldfinches, drab in winter attire, their feathers tarnished like forgotten silver.

Meals change. The fragrant fresh salads of summer fade into heavy root vegetables; charbroiled chops into hardy stews and soups. Oatmeal with maple syrup for breakfast; muffins for tea. There's a bearish quality to edibles and exertion; a fat layer insinuates to insulate for winter.

Light dwindles. Dark mornings pair with dark evenings, closing in like bookends on a depleted shelf. Each day, a few more minutes fall away until eventually my trips to the barn are dark. I leave the light on in the coop for Maureen and Lucy between chores. Hens are photoperiodic; they lay when the days are long. They fall for the ruse and continue to provide eggs each day.

I find it harder to rise in the mornings with less to do outside, with unwelcome weather to greet me. A sunrise clock helps, its crescendo glow mimicking a rising sun, but set to begin hours before the light appears. Fickle dawn reluctantly rises in murky grey, her rosy fingers stuffed deep in pockets of cloud. It will turn out to be the greyest November on record. Daylight saving will soon be over. What little light there is at dusk will now disappear, detoured to the wan morning.

In other years, by now I would be readying the ewes for breeding. Two to three weeks before the ram goes in, I augment their feed with whole oats at the evening chore. Over a week, I increase the amount to about a pound a day per ewe in order to encourage extra ovulation with this rising plane of nutrition. The process is known as flushing, and we do it to encourage multiple births. But since I've decided to delay lambing this time, hoping for better weather next May, the ewes are on maintenance. Just hay.

As well as shifting lambing, we will also replace our ram. All the dilemmas of the year — the difficult lambings, the losses, the barren ewes, the ineffective ram — have culminated in the need for a new sire, a new tup for the flock. Hunter has been with us a good few years, and it is time for his genes to carry on elsewhere. It is always difficult to change rams. He is half the flock. But in other years, I've been successful in finding new homes for older rams, and it is time for him to go. It is difficult to find new blood for Border Leicesters; they are not a popular breed in an era where meat and synthetics trump wool as a cash crop. Hunter is from a prize flock whose genetics dominate the breed. Good genes to be sure, but comingled. We decide to go farther afield and contact a shepherd in Quebec.

Johanne is a dedicated sheep farmer in the Montérégie region whose tenacity overwhelms me. She has an enormous flock — hundreds of animals — and a long heritage of sheep farming. Her focus is on meat production, and her operation is based on a three-way cross, the gold standard for hybrid vigour and carcass quality. To do this, she keeps three separate flocks: Romanovs, for their prolificacy and out-of-season fertility, Border Leicesters for their excellent mothering and milking, and Hampshires for their growthiness and muscle. She breeds them all true, then crosses the Romanov dams with Border Leicester sires for ewes, and crosses them a final time with Hampshire rams for market lambs. Her operation is a marvel of management.

To extend her bloodlines, she imports animals from afar, and this is what intrigues us. Her Border Leicesters from Australia have no connection with our dwindling Canadian stock, which gives us the opportunity to breed new genes into our flock. In November, we set out to pick up our new yearling ram, barrelling down the highway in the pickup, our homemade stock racks installed. It's a long journey. Kathryn fills in as nanny to our flock, and we spend the night in a nearby town, enjoying the beautiful old stone buildings and the setting by the Richelieu River. We use our rusty French at dinner and have the most wonderful meal, feeling a pang for having left Quebec after university so many years ago to farm in Ontario.

In the morning, we arrive early at the farm, where the ram, who will be called Louis, is separated and ready to be moved. We have named him after the Richelieu River, changing *lieu* to *Lou*, and realize we will need to speak to him in French until he adjusts to life in English Canada. He's a massive animal but gentle, friendly. We make the trip home as quickly as possible to lessen his stress, but when we stop periodically to give him water and hay, we find him relaxed, lying quietly and comfortably in the straw on the truck bed.

It is the actual date for setting the clocks back after daylight so the rush is on to get home before dark. We just make it and back the truck up to the south door of the barn, where his pen is ready. Though he went on the pickup quite easily, Louis is very reluctant to get out. We tempt him, we encourage him, we try a gentle push. Nothing. I bring oats, a sure thing to move a sheep, but he is unimpressed. As the sky darkens and the time extends, we are at our wit's end as to how to get him off the truck. He's curious but unmoveable.

Finally, in utter frustration, I let the ewes out into the open area of the barn. They are excited to spill into the empty space, and they begin to dance, prance, and vocalize their glee for whatever excitement lies ahead. Louis sees them, he hears them, he jumps off the truck! They nose each other through the gates for a few minutes before I usher the ewes back to their side, and Louis finds his own feeder, his own well-bedded pen. We soothe him with our best French, pet him and nuzzle his neck, and leave him to settle in after a long journey.

He spends the rest of the month acclimatizing, learning our ways, eating our hay, adjusting to a new life at Lambsquarters until the day comes, at the very end of November, when we release him into the flock to begin his life's work.

火.犬

A bit of colour remains in the woods, where the aspen leaves form an Ezra Pound poem in shades of ochre and green and Naples yellow in tear-shaped dollops on the wet forest floor. There are deer at the edge of the wood, four of them who, because of a bitter east wind, are unaware of my approach from the west. The tamaracks are on fire, like the golden spruce, and contrast with the cedars, who have just dropped their russet fronds to glow a deep and vibrant green.

As the days diminish, snow alternates with rain and a wily west wind blows me toward the woods, impedes my return. Sections of the path are scraped clean — wild turkeys — though first I thought it could have been melted patches from resting deer. But no, the arrowhead marks of the turkey tracks are clear in the snow as I continue on to the next bend and there they are: thirty or forty of them, waddling leisurely away from me into the bush.

On the last day of hunting season, a neighbour spots me from his hide on the next farm. Wearing a high-vis vest to avoid being shot as I walk, I must look like a trespassing hunter, as he alerts another neighbour to call Thomas. He knows we discourage hunting on our land, and though he might also be concerned about competition close to his blind, it is a comfort to me. Neighbourhood watch.

Hunting is a tricky subject. I hate to see the deer killed, but I have been in a vehicle hit broadside by one and know many others who have been unable to avoid them on the road. They are terribly dangerous, suddenly running out from the bush at night into the path of cars, or immobilized by headlights coming around a curve or over a hill, the vehicle unable to stop. I love to follow their tracks and witness them following mine. The beauty of a fawn in spots; the power of a buck in full rack. The flash of the white flag of tails as they sail over fences, fly through thickets and away.

Coyotes, however, are a menace to sheep farmers, and we have had our losses. But they do a great job keeping rodents at bay, and if they don't eat my sheep, I'm happy to let them roam. I see their tracks almost daily once the snow flies, and occasionally we spy each other at a distance, stop, maintain eye contact, stand very still until one of us lopes away. For years, the hunters roamed the area until one day, when Thomas was working in the woods, their hounds rushed past him in full pursuit, followed by the men with guns. That was when we posted the property. I fear their weapons far more than the animals. But it marked us as other. Not letting the hunters in. Showing our towny background. Most of the No Hunting signs are gone now, rotted away, but the knowledge remains. Local hunters now wait until their prey cross the line fence. My neighbour in his blind got a buck when it left the land I steward and wandered into unsafe territory beyond. He did respect our wishes by not hunting on our land and by reporting what he thought was a trespasser. Our system worked well that day. If not for the deer.

Because I trust that respect, I do not stop walking during hunting season. I don an old orange down vest, really an orange-lined green vest I turn inside out. Either my son or my daughter picked it up years ago at some second-hand store when they still lived on the farm. They both grew out of it and handed it down to me. Little Mummy. It lives on a hook in the mudroom, just around the corner from the door frame that marks their heights at six-month intervals. From the time they could stand until they were full-grown, I measured them every birthday and half birthday, a ruler over the top of their heads, a pencil line, name, and date. My daughter first, then her brother, who slowly and quite remarkably overtook her and us all. So hard to believe that those babies I carried and delivered, fed and nurtured, watched take first steps, heard speak first words, sent to school and camp and university are now in their prime adult years. My daughter has children of her own; my son's adventures take him far away. But each November, I don the green vest inside out, flash the orange lining, and venture off to the sounds of gunfire, the sight of farmers who celebrate the annual break between harvest and calving, who have time to bond, to share exploits, to trudge through the rain and snow in pursuit of the most basic and ancient of activities. Who am I to object?

In previous warmer autumns, the sheep have still been on pasture in November, vulnerable during hunting season. One year, we had strangers with guns on the home farm. They wounded a deer in our swamp, broke rails on a fence to pursue it, then slaughtered and butchered it quickly on the road, leaving a trail of blood and gore. The sheep were just the other side of the fence, terrified, grouped in a huddle like muskoxen, the lambs surrounded by their dams. I've kept them closer since then, and this year they are safe, I hope, within the courtyard of the barn, protected by stone walls, access to cover. When they hear a gunshot, they immediately stop eating or ruminating and look up in unison, their eyes pointing toward its echo, their ears pricked in alarm.

Birds make themselves scarce when the hunters arrive. Or lift in a flock to veer away. Skeins of starlings braid the air going south, stopping for breath to blacken the tops of cedars, squawking and cackling before they lift again in a Mobius scarf. Geese vee their way warmer, gliding and honking; trails of ducks follow in a constant flap. Roosting turkeys bend the upper branches of the maples, content to do a balancing dance until a shot rings out and they take to the sky like Hercules airplanes. Their lumbering bodies slowly and noisily lift off with ungainly wings flapping wildly.

Then one day the biggest avian hunter of them all, a magisterial bald eagle, holds court from the top of a white pine. Crowning the crown of the tree, all of creation held in its Hughesian foot, it reigns above the hunters, above the prey, its white head a beacon of strength and power. Once plentiful near the Great Lakes, eagles were ravaged in the last century. The widely used pesticide DDT weakened their eggs. The shells broke prematurely; the chicks died. The eagles are increasing again, though still threatened by development along the lakes, so a sighting is a rare treat. With luck, this one will find a partner and make a nest come spring. Its shadow in flight obliterates large swaths of the ground it surveys; its wingspan can stretch over two metres.

As the weather worsens and the birds deplete, the tamaracks too are giving up the ghost. Deciduous conifers, they are balding, skeletal, as they drop their needles to carpet the forest floor in brilliant raw sienna, quinacridone gold. It's a last flash of colour after all the leaves are gone, the oval poplars turning black on the ground sprinkled over with dun oak leaves, their colours morphing to mere shape. Incongruously, the field glows green as the winter wheat germinates up through the remnants of previous corn stover and bean trash. A couple of centimetres high, it has established its roots and will coast there until the seasons change and trigger further flourish.

By mid-month, the snow flies in earnest. Everything is white; branches once high now weigh down, sweep into my hood, and sprinkle me with snow. The turkeys are back in the field, Brobdingnagian black blobs digging and pecking, scratching like giant hens to get at the grains below, the tiny shoots of wheat. Deer tracks, in tandem, reassure me that some have survived the rifles' onslaught.

The corn beyond has yet to be cut. Too wet to harvest earlier, not yet cold enough for the ground to freeze and support the combine. It is a very late season, threatened by pink mould, which is rampant down country. But the great southwest is lower, wetter, less well-drained. The mould is a type of fungus that produces a toxin called deoxynivalenol, or DON. It can be harmful to animals, so the grain elevators won't accept corn if the DON levels are too high, and the ethanol companies and distilleries are reluctant to take it if they can't sell the by-product. The farmers here are wary, fingers crossed that the cold weather will continue, that the ground will freeze, that they can finally harvest a fruitful crop.

Most years, corn covers more than two million acres in Ontario. It is used primarily for animal feed (which anyone from the city who has ever stolen a few tough bitter cobs to eat will know) and as biofuel. Some of the crop is cut early as silage, but most is harvested for the kernel, either for fodder or manufacture. Cornstarch and corn syrup thicken and sweeten countless foodstuffs, but corn has other less obvious uses in chewing gun, envelope adhesive, paper cups, toothpaste, chalk, talcum powder, table salt, matchsticks, crayons, and much more. But only if the farmer can get it off the field.

It still provides cover for the coyote, whose tracks veer off the snowy road and into the stalks. Stalking. The days follow dull and grey, the snow a trudge on my walk but not quite deep enough to ski. The trees are frosted, but with no sun to make them sparkle, they just look scary — frozen fingers.

The few lambs I kept are scouring. Why, all of a sudden? They are on dry feed; they have nothing obvious to make them loose; worms should be dormant by now. They aren't anaemic; their conjunctivae are pink and healthy. I spread fresh straw, call the vet. Coccidiosis, she says, but will analyze a sample to be certain. This is something I've never seen before, though apparently it is ubiquitous. Perhaps the wet weather has caused a proliferation. I read that sun, heat, and dry conditions control the oocytes. All in short supply this month. Indeed the test is positive: I must drench for five days. By day four, I see improvement; there are pellets in the pen. I determine to read up on this parasite and consider preventive treatment in next year's lambs, marvelling that I'm still discovering new problems after all these years. Lifelong learning.

It is finally time to flush the ewes before breeding. They are delighted with their evening sprinkling of oats, as is Louis, still in his separate pen. I increase the amount slowly over the week so they acclimatize, as we've had enough upset digestive tracts in the lambs. To tidy them and clean up the lambs, we hire a pair of shearers to crutch the flock. This involves shearing the wool from between the hind legs and around the tail area. Basically, an ovine Brazilian.

Our regular shearer has been ill, quite gravely, though we understand he is recovering. We book two young men, brothers Jake and Sam, to do the job. We've watched them shear at the annual contest each year, timed their progress, and admired their improvement since they first began. Of course, they've been taught by an expert — our regular guy. They've never been to Lambsquarters before, and they are anxious to come and clearly aim to please. We are delighted with their work and sorry for the scoury lambs, which they accept with aplomb. They are careful, kind to the animals, and concerned with cleanliness; they disinfect their equipment between flocks. The animals dance off, bits of loose fleece fringing their backsides, but clean and tidy, sprightly now they are free of their dags. Louis will have an easier time of breeding, and shearing will be cleaner come spring.

※ ※

There's a single mallard duck at the entrance to the woods. As I approach slowly on my arduous walk in slushy snow, she flutters around and skids a bit before waddling into the forest and out of sight. A lone duck. Why? And where will she go by herself? Has she been left behind? Too slow to keep up? Too old? On a metaphoric ice floe? Here we are, two old birds together fighting against time, against the onset of winter, against the inevitable decline of the season, of life.

I do not see her the following day. And I am still here, walking doggedly, doglessly, before or after my barn chores, hunting for stragglers, for tracks, for signs. The lambs are recovered; Louis is calm. Yvette, my oldest ewe, looks thin. She has a cough. I watch her closely to be sure she gets her ration of oats, leafy hay. Then just when it seems the sky will be dark for months, there is a sudden glimpse of sunrise. A thin line of palest yellow topped by rose blush blended into the soft grey. A slight promise of light. A red-bellied woodpecker arrives at the suet feeder. I call him Rory.

The red morning sky warns of snow, and squalls arrive before the day is over. Louis's water pail is frozen solid. I bash the black rubber until the ice shatters and try to guess how much water he'll need at each feeding. If I calibrate it correctly, he will be adequately hydrated and I'll not have to deal with ice. The wind scurries through the fields, whisking the snow into dervishes, alternately clearing and drifting the terrain, making walking difficult, skiing impossible. Still I head out, not missing a day in some obsessive need to keep the pattern, like breathing, to stay alive. In the woods, out of the wind, I discover all the secret thoroughfares of wildlife. Big deer, little deer, one just ahead of me bounding through the bush, though I don't see it. Great spaces between its running hoof prints. Coyote, fox, rabbit, squirrel. My own field tracks are pure rumour by the time I return. Disappeared into the swirl.

After crutching, we put the coats back on the black ewes. It is fairly easy to get them off this time of year when they are not in full fleece. Thomas holds the animal, and I unbuckle the leg straps, then pull the coat up and over their heads. I can't resist saying "peek" as their heads reappear. Putting them back on is more problematic. In the past, Thomas has straddled the ewe while I put the coat over her head and then try to pull it down her back between his legs. There's scant space. It is difficult for me and precarious for him. A kind of intimacy nobody really enjoys. My hands seize up in the cold, my joints complain, my trigger finger locks in the off position.

We try another way. Instead of straddling the ewe, Thomas holds her against the wall, one knee under the chin, the other in front of the flank. I pull the coat over the animal's head, slide it down her back, and reach under to attach the near hind leg strap. If possible, I reach through to the far leg; if not, I have Thomas turn the ewe around. It works. The ewe is well controlled; I needn't wiggle thick canvas through a tight space; there is no climbing involved. Just creaking knees as I crouch and rise, crouch and rise, more slowly now than in the past. It's miserable again outside, soggy wet snow and dark skies, so I keep them inside and feed them where it's dry.

Heavy snow follows, builds, lasts all night. There is enough for me to get out my skis. Slow to begin, I gain a rhythm and find myself sailing along like a younger version of myself. I'm using different muscles, my arms busy with the poles, my legs pushing and gliding, but it feels good. Fast. Next day, there are deer tracks parallel to my trail. We are tandem travellers on different shifts.

The final day of November belongs to Louis. It is his day to join the ewes. Separated in the barn, they have spoken, exchanged pheromones, but not yet met. We are anxious: he is an untried ram and our whole year's crop depends on his performance in the next few weeks. Border Leicester sheep will cycle for only about four months, starting when the days are getting shorter. Because I am hoping for better lambing weather, I have waited an extra month to put the ram in, and he must act quickly to catch the ewes before their oestrus stops. I hope I have chosen well. He has a large scrotum, uniform and evenly balanced testicles. Although I didn't actually get down with my measuring tape, which is advised when selecting a ram, I did manage a good palpation, satisfying myself that his anatomy is intact and promising, with no abnormalities. His testicles did not feel excessively hot, nor were they swollen. The epididymis at the base of each was firm but not excessively hard, indicating good fertility. I likely should have done a proper measurement, but I feel confident that Louis ranks above the minimal scrotal circumference of thirty centimetres.

There are so many variables, so many aspects to choosing a ram. And unfortunately so few to choose from in this breed. The wool is important to me, and though he was not in full fleece when I first saw him, I was pleased with the crimp and uniformity. He did not have heavy, hairy, wavy wool on the britch, a common flaw of hindquarter wool in a country that does not highly value its clip. A ram must have strong legs and feet. To breed, he must be comfortable and balanced on his hind legs. And overall conformation is crucial to good quality progeny. The mouth must be even, neither over- nor undershot so the teeth directly meet the hard palate. Shoulders should be large and solid, the bones well connected and strong, the chest deep, the pasterns short and wide, and the limbs straight and in line with the shoulders and hips. A leg in each corner, they say. The back and rump should be straight, not sagging or humped.

Each breed has specific characteristics and particular flaws. Border Leicesters must have black noses; a pink nose is unacceptable, not just ugly. Their hooves also must be black. I prefer to see black eyeliner, but it is not a necessity, and Louis is rather short on kohl. Purely aesthetic, it has no effect on meat or wool production. I just like the look.

He is the ram we have, the one we've chosen from a small offering, and the only one I could find with outside bloodlines. Today is the day to see if he is ready to work. Past rams have broken out of their pens to get in with the ewes. Louis is more relaxed, which makes me anxious. When he is set free, he is composed, chats up the ewes, who mill about him, who go after him unabashedly, tripping over each other to make friends, make lambs.

He takes his time, chuckling, nudging, moving around among the flock before choosing his mate. I witness a connection, a definite breeding, and walk away, leaving them to it, giving them space, privacy. He's calm, and as long as he knows what to do (and does it), I can only be pleased at his demeanour. No jostling at the feeders, no bunting others away; he is a gentle addition to a quiet flock. Time will tell if he's up to the task.

December

Despite the darkening days, the colder nights, there is a small shift in mood when the calendar turns to December. There are three more oppressive weeks for daylight hours to shrink further, and three more before we are back to what little light we have now, but there is a sense of hope in the air. Hope that the rain and slush will turn to flaky snow. That the moon will shine brilliantly through the trees when it rises. Hope that crisp days will produce sun dogs, parallel rainbow parentheses around the sun, or that nights will bring lunar halos when light bends and refracts through high icy clouds.

I've learned to read the sky living here. From hot August days lying on the truck bed to watch the Perseid meteor showers, to evening chores in December when the stars break through. Venus, Cassiopeia, Orion's belt; the north star static, a constant polar point above the barn; majestic Ursa Major circling with respect. And aurora borealis. In the early days, we saw northern lights frequently, dancing over the barn roof, sashaying above the hay-field on moonless nights. But light pollution has reached us now. Neighbours burn yard lights all night long. Nearby towns are ablaze, and even the sleepy village has put up a despicably bright sign that projects for miles. There are red-lit telephone towers and wind towers not far off. All blinking, obliterating the night sky.

As city lights encroach, as city dwellers move closer and replicate their suburban street lamps, offending my precious darkness, there are also lights disappearing. Missing, like their owners. I watched the farmhouse to the south pulled down and burned. Their kitchen light, a comfort for years that a neighbour was not far away, has been put out forever. The farmer was the last of a long family line to farm that land since colonization seized it from Indigenous hands. He ambled along in his old truck, his old tractor, dressed in his uniform of striped overalls and cap, checking his cattle and fences down the way, sometimes stopping for a chat. And the reluctant farm wife walked through the fields with presents for my babies when they were born. A teddy bear is still around somewhere. Blue Ted.

In our early days, we saw them harvest their grain the old way, stooks dotting the field. There were lush fencerows then, parallel lines of maples and hawthorns dividing the field, all gone the way of the threshing machine that sorted their wheat from the chaff. Many more bushels of wheat grow there now, but what have we lost with the husks?

To the west, we no longer see our neighbour's lights for the trees. Cedars, just small when we arrived, now tower along our fenceline, altering the view. Old pictures attest to the dramatic change. I've been here that long. The trees are old now. I am old.

To the north, the house is dark, Maik and Gerrit, who were so much a part of our lives, who taught us so much, are now dead and gone, the farm abandoned, forlornly waiting for someone new. Eastward, beyond the neighbour's cultivated fields, where once I skied around a natural wetland, there's now a twee pond, a modern house, a professional landscape, a harsh city light burning all night.

Much as I crave a dark night sky, I acquiesce to some artificial evening light. Trips to the barn, even as early as five o'clock in the afternoon, are dismal in December. I just want to get there, feed out, and get back. At that time of day, lights can help. I put timed spotlights on the house, fairy lights in my white garden, strings of clear bulbs on the obelisk by the barn. All snow and ice (or melting muck), the garden is dormant but for a few carrots buried under straw for winter harvest. Rustic cedar posts with angled crossbars and dried grape vines, the obelisk towers over me. I need a ladder to string the lights from the top, then wind them around and around like a maypole until they shine out in a cone, a tree. They greet my trip to the barn, light my return. Then switch off for a dark night.

December's diminishing daylight is particularly cruel following the darkest November on record. The sun rarely broke through; precipitation fell almost daily. We were sun-starved in a typically dreary month.

The sheep seem happier than I feel. Louis, though calm, is clearly enjoying his time among the ewes. And they vie for his attention, all but batting their eyelashes as they sidle up to his neck. There's no serious risk of anthropomorphizing when I witness some of their antics. If a ewe is interested in breeding, she squats down and urinates in front of the ram. Louis finds this attractive; he curls his upper lip, raises his nose, and deeply inhales the offered pheromones. The ewe might coyly move away before squatting again in an ongoing mating dance until she decides to acquiesce and stand for him. He chuckles and approaches her sideways at first, rubbing necks, lifting a foreleg against her flank. After this foreplay, he mounts in earnest, makes a few short thrusts, and almost falls back, spent. They continue as a couple for a time, often repeatedly breeding. She eventually wanders off back to the feeders, and Louis, after a short dénouement, sniffs around for his next true love. When he's excited, he sometimes approaches ewes who are not ready, not yet interested in what he has to offer. He follows them around the feeders, persuasive, even insistent, but unless a ewe stops and agrees, no breeding takes place. She is ultimately in charge. He cannot hold her.

Of course, I contemplate the consequences of their actions, though I doubt they occur to the sheep. As a farmer, I want conception. I've fed extra to encourage more twin pregnancies, and I want all my ewes covered. None left "open." I realize it is a choice I have not given them, whether to breed or not. I oblige them to go through yearly pregnancies, lambings, separations. They succumb to the urge and suffer the results. Their fierce protection of newborn lambs every spring softens my concerns. Though the ewes must deal with the physical conditions of reproduction, they have no cultural judgments or expectations to face. They blithely accept the ram's attentions and get on with their day, eating, breeding, gestating. It is my responsibility to determine their future, and I try not to take it lightly.

Louis, big and beautiful, is not an aggressive breeder. We've had rams in the past who bully the ewes — not by forcing themselves but by worrying them at the feeders, chasing them away from their food, bunting, and generally bothering. I'm particularly wary of these macho guys. Louis has shown none of these characteristics, and I can safely walk among the flock without incident. Since I no longer use a crayon attached to the ram's brisket with a harness, all I can do is watch, hope, and wait until it's possible to ultrasound the dams to determine Louis's potency. And that can't happen for almost three months. It's a big risk. A year's crop.

※.※

On the sixth of December, I travel out of my farm life for the day. I'm still physically here, but my mind is in Montreal, where I was an undergraduate so many years ago, and in Hamilton where I was in a university classroom at the moment fourteen women students were murdered at École Polytechnique because they were women. It doesn't visibly resonate around here, but I've no doubt everyone who is reminded of the event is given pause. I pin a white ribbon to my coat, wear a commemorative pin, carry around a list of their names in my pocket, and at some point in the day I say them each aloud. It is a time I miss the feminist supports of my past city life, when I feel detached from my bucolic isolation in the country, when I feel alone in remembrance. Every two and a half days, a woman or girl is killed in Canada. It is difficult not to despair.

※.※

The dark days and the dark thoughts are mitigated somewhat by the season itself. Rural Ontario is, regrettably, still largely culturally homogenous, so Christmas is celebrated with vigour. Avoiding the commercial aspect so prevalent elsewhere, the village holds an annual non-motorized parade where a menagerie from equine and canine to ovine and avian either pull or adorn floats up Main Street. It's been going for years now and attracts hundreds of people who line the sidewalks, bundled up against the snow, drinking cocoa, marvelling at the heavy horses, their brasses glowing, their tails and manes braided; the dogs with antlers attached; the chickens and bunnies in wagons pulled by small children. Farmers trailer their animals from counties away just for the pleasure of showing them off. They have nothing to sell. Nothing to display but their pride.

We always stand in the same place, just at the base of the hill across from the feed mill, and frequently we witness a horse, and once a whole team, slipping on the slick snowy road. Everyone rushes back if the horses buck. Everyone except those brave and competent few who rush forward and grab the harnesses, calm the animals, get them back in line.

Each year, there is something new: miniature horses, dressage, high steppers, a sheep coloured red and green. This year, some of the beasts have sparkling snowflakes stencilled on their flanks; others gleam with tiny flashing lights.

It's the sound that affects me most. Unlike town parades, blasting canned music and fire sirens, much of the village parade is completely silent but for the clip-clop of the horses. Huge Clydesdales with shining furry spats have massive horseshoes tapping octaves lower than the sleek riding horses, whose hooves ping on the tarmac, their mounts red-cheeked and sassy, weaving from one side of the road to the other, throwing candy to the kids.

But the bells are the best. Ancient sleigh bells, handed down from generations of horse folk, grace the traces and harness of the teams. It's a sound like no other, instigating nostalgia in a collective unconscious, for how many of us could have an actual memory? Even I am not old enough for that. But the children here will grow up knowing what their great-grandparents heard in their youth, keeping the past alive and evoking for me a song by Lightfoot, a poem by Frost. More bells jingle as an open sleigh passes by, drawn by a single mare.

For years, the general store was the centre of events, welcoming shivering clients, supporting school trippers selling hot drinks to raise their fare. It's had various owners since we've been here, the best, the better, and the good. But for the past while, it has been ugly. A new owner seemed antagonistic to the clientele, booting out the old guys from their morning coffee klatch, tearing down the sign that announced everyone's birthday, calling the police on mischievous schoolboys. One by one, the residents were insulted, abused, or just disgusted until it seemed almost no one went in. Instead of being the centre of the community, what we previously called the local "mall," its parking area emptied, its blinds drew down, its hours diminished. Everyone despaired of losing the store, but no one wanted to go there to keep it going. It is the only sad note to the parade.

But in the crowd, there are faint murmurings that it might come up for sale, rumours that descendants of the most convivial owner, who made us so welcome when we arrived here many years ago, are thinking about taking it on, bringing it back to full feather. There is hope in the crisp air.

Up the road in the next township, a farmer conducts a concert in his barn. My daughter and I come in from the cold for Handel's Messiah with the cows. The dairy herd is across from us, beyond the orchestra and choir, their horns glistening in the low light, their cowbells ringing off-key and offbeat when they shake their necks. Every once in a while one bellows, complains perhaps at the baroque intrusion, but the music continues. We sing along from the score we brought with us, bouncing unabashedly from soprano to alto with the melody. Behind us is a calf pen, the animals close enough to touch, their warm bovine scent wafting over the gate to the beams where the hens roost, undisturbed by trumpets sounding. Cats amble nimbly through the maze of adzed timbers unperturbed, as if accustomed to a stable full of music and singing audiences. When it comes to a close, we exit silently as becomes the time and place. And once again the privilege of living here overwhelms me.

❦

In the dark days, I crave bread. I make loaves in a baguette pan, starting the dough in the evening — just flour, salt, water, a tiny bit of yeast — and let it proof overnight. In the morning, I form it into a ball, let it sit for a few minutes, then roll it into long cylinders for a final rise. As it bakes over a pan of boiling water, the kitchen warms and fills with scent.

I plan holiday food. Large shortbread rounds imprinted with a wooden mould in the form of a Scotch thistle. Edible heritage. Some years, I deliver them to the neighbours with jars of maple syrup. Everyone craves sweets in December. For Christmas Eve, I will make my own version of tourtière, a French Canadian meat pie. Instead of traditional ground pork, I use my own lamb, seasoned with thyme from the garden, thickened with potatoes from the root cellar, and moistened with homemade chicken stock. I can't do decent pie crust, but Thomas is an excellent pastry chef; he inherited his baker grandfather's skill and his rolling pin. With a Christmas tree cookie cutter, I cut out pastry scraps to decorate the crust, make a star in the centre for steam.

There will be beans and carrots preserved from the garden, peas perhaps, maybe squash, and for dessert, pavlova. I save the eggs until they are at least three days old and leave them to warm on the counter. Any fresher or colder and they won't beat into glossy peaks. I've frozen enough whole raspberries from the summer harvest to adorn the whipped cream on top. I am at one with the farm when I cook with ingredients grown on this land.

※.※

It snows and snows, brightens even the darkest days. The corduroy bridges in the woods, inaccessible in all the wet slippery weather of the fall, are finally passable again, the deep snow giving me purchase to cross. The deer have preceded me, their tracks crossing the stream where the coyotes made a path months before. And one morning, I see the fox. She's trotting along the farm lane, up behind the driveshed and into the hayfield and away. In no hurry, as if she does this every day, but only now, red against the pristine white, is she visible. With fresh snow, I'll see her tracks, keep track.

꙳ ꙳

The farm to the north has been sold. Empty for so long, paint-flaking house, empty echoing barn, it will breathe new life in the spring. A young Mennonite man will farm, keep cattle, work the land. Not waiting for possession, he is granted permission to till the soil in December. Fields that haven't seen a plough since the last century are to be turned and furrowed while the snow flies, readied to be planted when it finally melts away.

Few farmers hereabouts plough anymore. No-till planting has left rusting coulters, shares, and mouldboards disintegrating behind drivesheds. Ploughing turns over the weeds and plant residue from previous crops, but it also causes soil erosion, enhances run-off of fertilizers and pesticides, and delays drainage by ponding in the furrows. Ploughing is just the beginning of the cultivation process. Many more rounds on the tractor — with discs and harrows, seed drills and roller — entail far greater labour than no-till planting, and fuel costs can be up to 80 percent higher. It's disastrous for the planet. However, it is the traditional way, and Old Order Mennonites are traditional people.

One morning early, before dawn, just barely stirring awake, I'm aware of a bright light coming in the bedroom window. There is no road in view, so what is it? A meteor? A medevac helicopter?

I sit up and gaze out to see a tractor in the neighbouring field. The young man is ploughing in the dark. He worked through the day before and clearly wants to finish. Until he takes possession, he must travel a fair distance from his parents' farm, and like his brethren, he does not drive a car or truck. He must travel by horse and buggy, bicycle, or tractor. He has stayed overnight in the house, and once he gets the last field ploughed, he will drive the tractor home, secure in the knowledge that the fields have been prepared to his standard.

I admire his stamina, his commitment. I hope to get to know him and hope he will have a family eventually and that we will become good neighbours. I note the contrast from the other farmers in the block, from our farm, our way of life. I think for a moment, selfishly, about the cluster flies that insinuate themselves into the cracks in the bricks between the windows of the house. They emerge on warm winter evenings near the wood stove, or on sunny days, crowd into corners, buzz around lights. We have been less bothered with them since no-till, because, I surmise, the soil is undisturbed. By turning the soil over, the plough exposes both the earth and the earthworms; the flies lay their eggs in the fresh dirt and the larvae climb aboard the worms, parasitic until they pupate. They'll likely be back.

Change is harder as the years pile on. Our original neighbours altered little over the years they were there. Once their pension cheques started, they sold the Holsteins, closed down the milk house. Gone was the thick cream; no more honking horn to call in the cows from the back fields on hot summer evenings. But little else has changed. The fields stayed in permanent pasture, but for beef, not dairy. They were always open for me to meander; the stile at our line fence easing my way across.

Our new neighbour, once he finished ploughing, started cutting down the fencerows. He will make large fields, free of obstacles, and he will plant crops, not pasture animals. I fear for our borrowed landscape to the east. Two rows of mature trees that protect us, insulate us, shelter birds and beasts. I cherish these trees: hawthorns and wild apples that bloom in the spring, black cherries, maples. A whole history in bark and leaf in peril, threatening to expose me if clear-cut. Perhaps I'll ask him for a stay. A reprieve for ten years. Long enough to see me through.

And after I'm gone? No longer able to keep up with the work, no longer able to drive to town for supplies, no longer living? What will happen to the farm then? I can imagine the Mennonites enveloping the land, adding it to theirs, perhaps retiring one day to this house, or installing a son in a place of his own. That's most likely. The stone walls will collapse slowly.

But I harbour a specific succession wish. There is no chance of my own children farming. They love Lambsquarters, but they have other landscapes: lakes, mountains. Fields and meadows are their past, not their future. The grandsons, however, are as yet undetermined. They are young enough to influence, and I do my best to encourage their love of the land. Ever since they could walk, they've gone right in with the lambs, meeting them at eye level, holding out a hand to be inspected. When bigger, they could pick them up, hand-feed a bottle lamb, help a ewe to settle. And now they get right in and help with a difficult lambing, catch and hold a big labouring ewe.

They love to feed the sheep, at first standing on old milk crates to reach the feeders, then throwing hay by handfuls down into the outside mangers. Now they handle heavy bales — right at the same time that I find it difficult. I'll need their help, and I hope I've groomed them well.

This dream is unlikely, really. The farm is not big enough to support a family. And will their future choices allow for country life? The farm magazines are full of advice for succession. How to hand over the farm to a daughter, a son. But it is financial information, not emotional currency, they address. I've seen what happens to gardens gone derelict when the gardener dies or moves away. To old bank barns that have been abandoned when the last farmer sells out to agribusiness. And I maintain hope that my grandsons, Ian and Alistair, and possible future grandchildren, will keep this farm. In their hearts, if not with their hands.

The thought of passing it on — a chattel, property, something I own and have agency over — is distressing in itself. This is land improperly given, improperly taken, improperly bought and sold. I contemplate the possibility of giving it back.

I would not be the first to consider returning this land to First Nations members. Possibly to be stewarded by descendants of those who were relocated by my own great-great-great-grandfather. Almost thirty years ago, a farmer down country offered to share his farm with Anishinaabe Chippewas of Point Pelee who have no recognized property. They considered it too far away from their traditional lands; they declined the offer. But as I age and anticipate the succession of this farm, it is time to interrogate the possibilities for its future, including investigating the sacred bonds that Indigenous cultures have with the land — the treaty implications, the different approaches to land as either owned and exploited for economic gain or as a part of nature, like humanity itself, to be treated with reverence and respect.

With more farmers now over the age of seventy than under thirty-five, and with fewer youth interested or financially able to take over family farms, there is a concern that farmland is at risk. I'm one of the majority of farmers with no succession plan. There is growing interest in pairing farmers who have extra land — those getting too old to manage — with people seeking land to farm. Immigrants who have had to leave farms in their home countries, young people unable to raise enough money to buy land, city dwellers wanting to be closer to their food sources. The baby boom includes farmers: our large cohort will effect a huge rise in land transfer over the next number of years as we age out. But I'm not there yet. I will stay, breed my flock, shepherd them, bring lambs into the world, and inevitably send them off.

As I look out my farm window on a winter day, the clouds a mass of grey, the rolling hills and stone walls thick with snow, I think back to those idyllic summer weeks living without amenities in the west of Ireland. I reflect on the youthful hopes and strengths I had then, played out and realized ever since on a life lived close to the land. I recognize and celebrate the privilege. I embrace the joy. And although age may have withered me, shepherding offers infinite variety. I will watch over the fields and valleys, the hills and dry land, and persevere day by day, month by month, another shepherd's calendar year at a time.

Notes

A Holstein cow is a rare sight: "The Canadian Dairy Industry,"
Holstein Canada, www.holstein.ca/Public/en/About_Us
/The_Canadian_Dairy_Industry/The_Canadian_Dairy
_Industry.

Sometimes a stone: First published in *BRICK* 94, Winter 2015.

*Animals, however, account for the next most likely cause of morbidity
and mortality*: Canadian Agriculture Injury Reporting,
Agriculture-Related Fatalities in Canada (2016), 17.

Farmers expect to be injured and tend not to report: P.H. Cummings,
Statistics Canada Catalogue, no. 21 (1992), 8.

*The number of farmers over eighty in Canada has increased by 58
percent*: Canadian Agriculture Injury Reporting, 9.

*Accidental death rate of these older farmers exceeds the national
average by more than 40 percent*: Canadian Agriculture Injury
Reporting, 14.

The tweed must be "handwoven by the islanders": "Who We Are," Harris Tweed, harristweed.org/journal/who-we-are-2.

The duchess, Georgiana, "turned the upper glen into a playground for her rich friends": David Taylor, "From Badenoch to Badenoch, Part Two," *History Scotland* (September–October 2016), 35.

Most years, corn covers more than two million acres in Ontario: "Ontario Plants Record Corn Acres," Farms.com, August 12, 2022, farms.com/news/ontario-plants-record-corn-acres -183356.aspx.

With more farmers now over the age of seventy than under thirty-five: Jessica Smith Cross, "Aging Farmers with No Succession Plans Put Future of Canadian Family Farms at Risk," The Canadian Press, July 16, 2017, cbc.ca/news/canada/toronto /family-farm-aging-farmers-canada-1.4207609.

Acknowledgements

For encouragement and assistance I would like to thank Maud Bruce; Anne Collins; Annie Garten; Robert Macfarlane; Margot Waddell; my agent, Jessica Woollard, at DHA; and my editor, Jen Knoch, at ECW.

My thanks to the Canada Council for the Arts for awarding me a Research and Creation Grant.

And finally I would like to pay homage to R.F. Karrow, Dorothy Knight, Richard Porritt, Thos Wilson, and watchful shepherds everywhere.

For every book sold, 1% of the cover price will be donated to the Grey Bruce Women's Centre, which provides secure shelter, crisis intervention, safety planning, counselling, and transition services for women and children affected by abuse in Grey and Bruce Counties.

This book is also available as a Global Certified Accessible™ (GCA) ebook. ECW Press's ebooks are screen reader–friendly and are built to meet the needs of those who are unable to read standard print due to blindness, low vision, dyslexia, or a physical disability.

At ECW Press, we want you to enjoy our books in whatever format you like. If you've bought a print copy or an audiobook not purchased with a subscription credit, just send an email to ebook@ecwpress.com and include:

- the book title
- the name of the store where you purchased it
- a screenshot or picture of your order/receipt number and your name

A real person will respond to your email with your ePub attached. If you prefer to receive the ebook in PDF format, please let us know in your email.

Some restrictions apply. This offer is only valid for books already available in the ePub format. Some ECW Press books do not have an ePub format for us to send you. In those cases, we will let you know if a PDF format is available as an alternative. This offer is only valid for books purchased for personal use. At this time, this program is not offered on school or library copies.

Thank you for supporting an independently owned Canadian publisher with your purchase!